P9-CAL-716

What People Are Saying About Moments

"Mike is a great story teller, and that'll be obvious when you open *Moments*. He pays such great attention to detail, and that comes from his genuine interest in his subjects. In this book, he has taken some people's very personal moments and turned them into opportunities to teach, inspire, motivate, and encourage. And that's a gift!"

- Ernie Johnson, Jr
Sportscaster, TNT/TBS

"As a consultant and coach myself, I know when I see a great one. Mike Van Hoozer is the real deal! This book captures his contagious energy, his ability to frame the eternal in practical and relevant language and stories, and his rock-solid character. Most of all, this book reflects Mike's pattern of relentless focus on the success of others, not on himself. If high integrity means no gap between what a person says and does, this book has ultimate integrity."

- Scott Kauffmann
Executive Director, Redeemer Labs

"In *Moments*, Mike Van Hoozer takes you on an easy, yet candid and entertaining exploration of the most important times of our lives: defining moments. *Moments* brightly unpacks the process of identifying the strategic inflection points in your life journey. These are the moments where success and failure are birthed. Read this book! Dare to identify the defining moments in your life and you will achieve your highest potential. Touchdown Mike!"

- Spencer Tillman
Author: *Scoring in the Red Zone*, CBS Sports Lead Studio Analyst

"In a moment life can change. We all have experienced such a time. Mike Van Hoozer brings us stories of profound and inspirational moments that changed lives, history, and eternity. I believe your life just might be altered if you take a "moment" to read this great book."

- **David Cook, Ph.D.**
One of America's Top Sports Psychologists and President, The Utopia Institute
Author: *Golf's Sacred Journey: Seven Days at the Links to Utopia*

"I feel honored and blessed to be profiled in Mike Van Hoozer's book. I had my 'Moment' while traveling in Argentina in 2006. I went to Buenos Aires to learn to play polo, but when I returned to the States, I had 200 pairs of shoes stuffed in my duffel bag and the idea to start a business that would forever change my life. Because of my 'Moment,' I just returned from South Africa where TOMS Shoes gave 50,000 pairs of shoes to children in need! I hope that everyone who reads this book is inspired to take action. Listen to Mike... we can change the world!"

- **Blake Mycoskie**
Founder and Chief Shoe Giver, TOMS Shoes

Moments:

Making Your Life Count For What Matters Most

Mike Van Hoozer

Insight Publishing
Sevierville, TN

Copyright © Mike Van Hoozer, 2008

10 9 8 7 6 5 4 3 2

ISBN 10: 978-1-60013-235-3
ISBN 13: 1-60013-235-9

All rights reserved. No portion of this publication may be reproduced, stored in a retrieval system, or transmitted in any form by any means - electronic, mechanical, photocopying, recording, or any other style - except for brief quotations embodied in printed reviews, without the prior written permission of the publisher.

Printed in the United States.

Insight Publishing
647 Wall Street
Sevierville, Tennessee 37738

To my loving wife Gina and our five wonderful boys.

Thanks for all of the memories and moments so far!

Table of Contents

Acknowledgements ix

Introduction xiii

Chapter 1   *The Meaning of a Moment* 1

Chapter 2   *A Defining Moment* 15

Chapter 3   *A Missing Moment* 35

Chapter 4   *A Disappearing Moment* 51

Chapter 5   *A Mountaintop Moment* 65

Chapter 6   *A Valley Moment* 83

Chapter 7   *A Courageous Moment* 103

Chapter 8   *A Powerful Moment* 117

Chapter 9   *A Purposeful Moment* 129

A Call to Action 153

Resources 161

About the Author 163

Acknowledgements

I have been impacted, encouraged, and challenged by many people over the years that have influenced the writing of this book. Their invisible hand of leadership is now flowing from my life to yours, and I thank them for their active presence in my life.

To my beautiful and precious wife Gina, you have made my life a great adventure. I am grateful for your love, your encouragement, your voice of challenge in my life, and your strong will.

To My Starting Five: Drew, Will, Kyle, Ben, and Grant. Thank you for your uniqueness and teaching me how to be a better father and a better leader through the experience of our lives together. I am so blessed to be your dad!

To my mom, I am grateful for your prayers and for making so many sacrifices to help me become the man I am today.

To Terrence Gee, the first real business leader and mentor I ever met. Thanks for your influence, your resolve, and your example. While I have told you many times, I will never forget your impact on my life.

To David Cook, thanks so much for teaching me the principles of the psychology of human performance. I have learned so much from you in a short period of time, and your servant's heart has touched the lives of many people, some of which you will never know.

To Spencer Tillman, I am grateful for our friendship and your example of living life with a passion and purpose and being intentional in every moment. Stay strong and stay faithful!

To Scott Kauffmann, a man of conviction and calling, who is not afraid to step out in faith. Thanks for inspiring me to do the same.

To Coach Holman, my high school basketball coach. Your example of leadership remains in my head and heart today. Because of you, I will never settle for anything less than my very best!

To Barry Landrum, my father-in-law and pastor. Thank you for your inspiration and for serving and loving others. You have made me laugh and think deeply, sometimes in the very same moment.

To Ernie Johnson, thank you for agreeing to share your story with me so that I could share it with the world. You are a living testimony of the journey of life.

To Blake Mycoskie, thanks for agreeing to share your moments with me. Your courage to step out in faith will continue to impact the world for generations to come.

To Orlando Palmeiro, thank you for your servant's heart and for all you did during our times together in Houston with the Astros. I will always remember the time we shared with your teammates, encouraging each other to fulfill our purpose and use our platform wisely.

To Steve Wilburn, thank you for your friendship and encouragement to follow my dreams. Your friendship has been invaluable to me.

To Matt Watson, your friendship has been incredible through our many journeys together in business and in life. May you always strive to continue being the kind of father, husband, and leader who others can look up to.

To Pat, my grandfather. While you are no longer alive on this earth, I know you are looking down on this moment with pride. You stepped in and became the leader I needed at a critical time in my life, and, for that, I am forever grateful!

To Louie Giglio, a brilliant communicator and visionary, thanks for your friendship and the lessons you taught me as a inquisitive college student. I have truly learned from you how to follow wisdom beyond human imagination and seek less of me and more of Him.

To the wonderful crew at my local Starbucks – Gladys, George, and Christina – thanks for making an excellent mocha and providing incredible customer service! Your environment provided the perfect setting for me to create much of what is found on the pages of this book.

To Paul J. Meyer, thanks for taking a chance on me, even before you heard me speak, to lead a retreat for one of your companies. The reaction to the Moments concepts truly inspired me to put it into written form.

To Jeremy McCasland, a talented musician, dear friend, and co-creator. Thank you for encouraging me to engulf myself in Moments! It inspired me to press on over the last two years.

Introduction

Learn from the past, prepare for the future, and perform in the moment. I was five, and the divorce was final. He had gone, and the choice was up to me: Make the most of my life or be still in a bed of bitterness.

In this groundbreaking new book, I explore the meaning of a moment and challenge readers to make their lives count for what matters most. I explore the meaning of a moment and the wide variety of synonyms that people use to describe a moment such as a split second, a day, a season of life, and a lifetime. Through the use of stories, I illustrate how the legacy of our choices, attitude, and responses in a "split-second" moment can affect a moment of greater length like a season of life as well as future generations. I invite the reader on a journey of moments including my own personal story of growing up without a father to becoming the father of five boys. I also serve as a guide and offer six principles to help maximize the moments in your life and make your life count for what matters most:

- Focus on the Moment
- Enjoy the Moment
- Engage in the Moment
- Perform in the Moment
- Respond in the Moment
- Pray in the Moment

I have used these principles in my own life as well as the lives of business leaders, entrepreneurs, and amateur and professional athletes that I have been so privileged to work with and coach over the years. In the book, I also share stories that illuminate these concepts and principles. The stories are deeply personal and involve both trials and triumphs in my own life as well as stories of some of my clients who have transformed their lives by putting these principles into practice in order to perform in the moment. The theme of each chapter of the book focuses on a certain type of moment including defining moments, valley moments, mountaintop moments, missing moments, disappearing moments, courageous moments, powerful moments, and purposeful moments. These moments provide a perfect backdrop for the stories to come alive in the context of moments that everyone experiences at some point in their life. Some of the stories in the book include:

- The perseverance of a child whose father disappears
- The courage of a mother and the faith that sustains her
- The purpose of Ernie Johnson, a 3–time Emmy award winning broadcaster for TNT, and his journey through cancer
- The defining moment of Blake Mycoskie, founder and chief shoe giver of Toms Shoes, who creates a company with a mission of giving a pair of shoes to children in need around the world for every pair of shoes that you buy
- The courage of a professional baseball player who is sustained through moments of doubt about his dad's battle with cancer
- A person who finds comfort in the midst of a valley and is carried back to a mountaintop moment
- A business leader who transforms his life to be more than just an achievement zone

In this book, I explore the following questions:

- What is the most important thing I can do in this moment?
- What is the purpose of this moment?
- Who else is impacted by this moment?
- How do I respond in this moment?

My hope and prayer is that you will be encouraged and challenged to live a more fully engaged life as a result of reading this book. You have been given so many moments… but only so many moments. Who are you going to be, and what are you going to do in the moment?

1

The Meaning of a Moment

Michael had just won the biggest race of his life, shattering his own world record by a third of a second and winning the gold medal in the Olympics. He thought about all of the training he had endured. He was thrilled that the discipline, hard work, and focus had paid off and given him a quiet confidence to achieve his goals. Most people would have thought Michael had just completed the perfect race. Yet, there was a brief moment during the race that he wished he could have replayed. A brief stumble the third step out of the block made him question how much faster he could have gone.

Moments have meaning. The word *moment* is derived from the Latin word *momentum* defined as "movement or moving power." If you research the word *moment*, you will find that this powerful word has a diverse set of synonyms:

- A split second
- The blink of an eye
- An instant
- A minute
- An hour
- A day
- A chapter in your life
- A season of life
- A phase

- A decade
- A generation
- An age
- A millennium
- An era
- An epoch

All of these words can be used to describe the word *moment* - everything from a split second to an epoch. Maybe it's just me, but it seems like there is a very wide gap between a split second and an epoch. How could one word represent so many meanings? As I reflected on this question and the meaning of a moment, I pondered how a split second moment could impact an epoch. Or closer to home, it made me aware of how an instant in my life could affect generations to come.

Every one of us has a deep longing for moments. Moments in the spotlight. Moments of expression. Moments of meaning and purpose. Moments of impact. Moments where we provide value to those we love the most. Moments filled with potential and promise. Some people have more of these moments than others.

Why do we crave, desire, and remember moments so much? I believe it is because moments comprise everything. Our time. Our choices. Our decisions. Our thoughts. Our relationships. Moments encapsulate all of these components. When we think of a moment, we rejoice over how we invested our time wisely, or we lament the fact that we let the moment slip away.

Moments are filled with issues to be resolved, opportunities to be realized, and challenges to be met. When we consider moments, we say things like, "Remember the time, we went to ...." "I'll never forget the time you ...." Some moments are forever ingrained in our memory. Others wash away like castles on the beach carried out to sea. When we remember moments, we rarely consider the literal time that the moment took place. We don't say, "Remember the time you said ... at 2:06 p.m."

Over the years, the specific time becomes less significant as we recall the time of year, the season of life, what age we were, and the way the moment made us feel and how it impacted our future.

I first became aware of the power of a moment during the journey of growing up without a father. My mom shared with me a pearl of wisdom that has been tucked within my heart for my entire life:

> *"Mike, when all is said and done in your life, you won't necessarily remember specific days; but you will recall moments, and these moments will hopefully be memories of a life well-lived."*

Can you imagine an 8-year old boy hearing and reflecting on these words? It wasn't like all of the memories so far had been perfect. I had a mom who was forced back to work through no choice of her own. I was searching for male role models in my life. I definitely could have been paralyzed by some of the moments I had experienced so far; yet, a young child tends to live in and for the moment. Most 8-year olds don't feel trapped by circumstances. They dream big and feel like they can accomplish anything. Why do we lose this sense of adventure as we grow older and more mature? How do we forget the power and significance of moments in our lives?

We all have moments in life. Some moments we sleep, some we stumble, and some moments we soar. The decisions, choices, and responses we make in a moment produce momentum in our lives either to fly or to fall. Every moment counts! The question is: Do we make the most of the moments in our lives? And how do we respond when there is a brief stumble along the way?

For Michael Johnson, the 1996 Olympics was a defining moment – a moment that determined his place in history. Defining moments can also be moments that help us clarify our calling and give us meaning and direction in our lives. Have you ever had a defining moment? Most people have several defining moments in their lives. The trouble with defining moments is that you cannot predict the exact second that a defining moment will happen. You can, however, prepare for defining moments in your life. Michael had endured countless hours of sprints and time in the weight room for a moment that lasted less than 20 seconds. He had spent 10 years of his life to reduce his time by 1.5 seconds – the difference between mediocrity and excellence. How are you preparing for defining moments in your life?

The 1996 Olympics also represented a lost moment - the stumble out of the starting block he wished he could have gotten back. Have you ever had a lost moment? A moment you didn't make the most of? Most of us have had at least one lost moment in our lives. The challenge is not to dwell on the moment that was lost but make the most of the moment that you have now. Michael persevered through this lost moment and made the most of the bigger moment.

In his book, *Slaying the Dragon*, Michael Johnson compares our experiences in life to those of a sprinter:

> *"Success is found in much smaller portions than most people realize, achieved through the tiniest gradations, not unlike the split-second progress of a sprinter.... Life is often compared to a marathon, but I think it is more like being a sprinter: long stretches of hard work punctuated by brief moments in which we are given the opportunity to perform at our best."*

Moments mean something, but do they mean something to us? Do we handle them with the proper respect that they deserve? We can't take them for granted. So often in life, we treat the moments in our lives like the air we breathe. They are in infinite supply and will always be there.

Each day when we look into the mirror, two questions should confront, challenge, and occasionally convict us. The first question comes from the book *Every Second Counts* by Lance Armstrong, cancer survivor and seven-time cycling champion of the Tour de France. In his book, he considers the question of deciding how to live once you discover you are not going to die – his opportunity after surviving cancer. In the first few pages of the book, he poses this simple yet profound question:

"What is the highest and best use of myself?"

If we properly considered this question and the implications of the answer each day, we probably would live more focused and fully engaged lives.

The second question considers the unknown – the amount of time we have on this earth:

"Would I live my life differently if I knew I only had a short time to live?"

Why does it sometimes take a crisis to awaken us to live passionate and purposeful lives? We must fully grasp the meaning of moments and handle them with care. As you read this book and think about the moments in your life, I encourage you to ponder the following questions:

- What is the most important thing I can do in this moment?
- What is the purpose of this moment?
- Who else is impacted by this moment?
- How do I respond in this moment?

What is the most important thing I can do in this moment?

Learn from the past, prepare for the future, and perform in the moment.

We miss so many moments in our lives, because we lament the past and dream too much about the future. We must learn to live in the moment, enjoy the moment, and cherish the moments that we have been given. As a coach to executives, families, and amateur and professional athletes, I have the honor and privilege of working with people to help them reach their maximum potential. Many times, the past and the future become roadblocks to navigating through the current moment. The past and the future can be important vehicles to help us appreciate the current moment.

Regarding the past, have you ever heard the following comments – not from yourself, but maybe from a "friend of yours:"

- "Because of my bad past, I am destined to have a horrible future."
- "My best days were in college, and it has been all downhill from there."
- "I wish I could go back to being 29."
- "What happened to the good old days?"

The past can trap and lock in your potential to be your best. It can hinder you from realizing your strengths and passions. The past can be a burden that you carry around for a lifetime. Don't be chained to your past! I will discuss ways to unleash the chains of the past throughout this book. The key point to remember is that your past can be a powerful, productive force or a piece of destructive kryptonite – a crippling substance even to the great Superman – depending on how you use it. The choice is up to you.

Last summer, our family was driving through Little Rock, Arkansas. We approached a stoplight and saw an ambulance driving in the opposite direction. My boys noticed something odd about the way the letters were written on the front of the ambulance as opposed to the side of the vehicle. The letters seem to be the same for both words, but the word on the front of the vehicle was indecipherable while the same letters on the side of the vehicle clearly spelled "AMBULANCE." My oldest son asked me about this and wondered why the front of the vehicle would have an illegible word for such an important vehicle. As I began to respond to his question, the answer became clear to him. "Oh I get it!" he exclaimed. "The letters are different on the front of the vehicle so that you can read them clearly when you see the ambulance in your rearview mirror." Exactly! The question for all of us is: Do the moments in our lives and the lessons learned from them become clear when we look in the rearview mirror? Or, do we see a foggy, blurry, indecipherable mess?

Clarity can be a great thing. We should seek it more in our lives. But, how do we discover clarity? Ralph Waldo Emerson always greeted his friends with an awesome and thought-provoking question:

"What has become clear to you since we last met?"

It is a question that I often ask of my coaching clients, my friends, and my family. "What has become clear to you since we last met?" What are the data points in your life? What moments have you experienced? What have you learned from those moments? And who are you going to be and what are you going to do as a result of those moments? The past is a portal for progress. You must go through moments to experience moments.

The Future

The future can be an exciting and motivating force in our lives if we use it in the right way. The problem with the future is that it is unpredictable. We do not know what tomorrow holds; yet, we can spend so much mental and emotional energy solely on the future. Famous quotes heard from proud prognosticators include:

- "I wish I didn't have that test tomorrow."
- "Why did I agree to go out with him this Friday?"
- "I am so worried about tomorrow's meeting!"
- "I guarantee we will win tomorrow night's game!"
- "I will do that tomorrow."
- "I always have tomorrow."

Do we always have tomorrow? Does tomorrow always wait for us? Many emotions can be tied up into tomorrow. Worry. Anxiety. Stress. Doubt. Confidence. Arrogance. Predictability. Uncertainty. What does the future hold for you? I don't know. You don't know. So, why are you spending time worrying and trying to control something you have no control over?

The future can be paralyzing or propelling depending on how we use it. The future becomes paralyzing in two ways. The first way involves procrastination. We become complacent and constantly defer things to the future. My grandmother used to always challenge me to not "put off till tomorrow what I could do today." Wise words from a wise woman!

The second way in which we become paralyzed by the future involves our emotions and thoughts. Worry, anxiety, and stress about what may or may not happen in the future consume our mental and emotional energy. We create realities that don't exist. I once heard a person utter the following statement:

> *"My life has been filled with terrible things, most of which never happened."*

This person was letting worry and stress devour her ability to enjoy the moments in her life. She was being consumed by the future. A future that never happened according to her dire predictions. Focusing on the future in this way keeps us from experiencing and enjoying the moments in our lives.

Alternatively, the future can propel us to be our best. Much of the coaching that I do begins with creating a shared vision for the future and then developing goals to achieve this vision. The future becomes a motivating force that propels them to be and do their best every day. The moments in their lives become meaningful, because they are tied to a shared vision. My clients see how what they are doing today advances the ball toward the ultimate goal. How do you use the future? Is it paralyzing or propelling? Is it mesmerizing or motivating?

Moments have profound meaning and significant impact. When you think about the moments in your life, I challenge you to ponder the following question: What comprises a moment? The answer lies in the acrostic **CAR**:

- <u>C</u>hoice
- <u>A</u>ttitude
- <u>R</u>esponse

This acrostic can be used to navigate the moments in our lives. First, C stands for choice. In every moment, we have choices. In the midst of a moment, we can choose how we feel, what we think, what we say, and what we do. Based on our decisions, consequences will result from these choices. The consequences can be good or bad, impactful or inconsequential, powerful or paltry. The ability to choose is a powerful thing, and the meaning of a moment begins with the power to choose.

The second letter **A** represents the word *Attitude*. Chuck Swindoll said the following about attitude:

"The longer I live, the more I realize the impact of attitude on life. Attitude, to me, is more important than facts. It is more important than the past, than education, than money, than circumstances, than failure, than successes, than what other people think or say or do. It is more important than appearance, giftedness or skill. It will make or break a company... a church... a home. The remarkable thing is we have a choice everyday regarding the attitude we will embrace for that day. We cannot change our past... we cannot change the fact that people will act in a certain way. We cannot change the inevitable. The only thing we can do is play on the one string we have, and that is our attitude. I am convinced that life is 10% what happens to me and 90% of how I react to it. And so it is with you... we are in charge of our attitudes."

Attitude is everything when it comes to unlocking your true potential. Your attitude articulates volumes about you. We all know what a great attitude looks like; yet, it is sometimes very difficult to put it on. It has been my experience that a great attitude comes from within. A great attitude comes from a spirit within us that persists and permeates all of who we are and exhibits its characteristics in everything we do and say. In the midst of a moment, your attitude can determine whether you persevere or plunder, soar or stumble, laugh or cry, appreciate or abhor, succeed or sink.

The final letter in the **CAR** acrostic is **R**, which stands for Response. We can choose our response in the middle of a moment. Our response can be negative or positive. It can be defiance or defeat. We can respond with a resounding "I WILL!" or a reticent "I won't." Success or Failure can hinge on our response in a moment. Contribution and impact can stand in the balance, waiting anxiously for our initiative to kick in. In his book *The Seven Habits of Highly Effective People*, Stephen Covey discussed the ownership we have in our response to events in our lives:

> *"Our behavior is a function of our decisions, not our conditions.... Look at the word responsibility – "response-ability" – the ability to choose our response. Highly proactive people recognize that responsibility. They do not blame circumstances, conditions, or conditioning for their behavior. Their behavior is a product of their own conscious choice, based on values, rather than a product of their conditions, based on feeling."*

We will build upon this acrostic throughout the book. For now consider these key questions:

- What choices do you make in the moment? How do your decisions and choices affect the outcome of a moment? Do you always make the best choices when confronted with a moment?
- What is your attitude in a difficult or challenging moment? What would others say about your attitude? How would they describe it?
- How do you respond to challenging situations? Are you an "I WILL" or an "I won't" person? What does patience have to do with your response in a moment?

Moments are Divine & Eternal

There is a spiritual query within every one of us. You can choose to discover it or ignore it. Embrace it or reject it. The answer is found in the matter of a moment – your life. This book is a collection of moments that make up every person's life. This book is focused on helping you maximize the moments in your life. It is a narrative on the importance of moments – how they should be treasured, not trashed. It is a statement on the reality of some people's lives, which are lived in quiet desperation. It is a cry for consistency and integrity in living your life. It is a call to action to consider your purpose and passionately pursue it for a lifetime.

I am not a perfect person, nor do the stories in this book reflect the actions of perfect people. I, like you, am on a journey each day to get it right. To make the most of my days. To be in alignment with why I am here. To make my life count for things that will last. Our time on Earth is but a moment, and the world in which we live is filled with temporary things that cry out for our time, attention, and resources. I don't want to invest in temporary things. There are some days that I make my moments count. There are other days when I struggle to understand the importance, significance, and purpose of the moment.

In this book, I will examine 6 principles that will help you maximize the moments in your life:

1. Focus on the Moment
2. Enjoy the Moment
3. Respond in the Moment
4. Perform in the Moment
5. Engage in the Moment
6. Pray in the Moment

I have used these principles in my own life as well as the lives I have been so privileged to work with and coach over the years. I will share stories along the way that will bring these concepts to light. Some of the stories are deeply personal and involve both trials and triumphs. Other stories I have been indirectly involved with and highlight clients that have put these principles into practice. Still other stories are ones that you have seen happen before you – in the media, in your community, and in your own home.

We all have our moments. The key question is: How are we using the moments in our lives to build momentum in pursuing our purpose? My hope and prayer is that the information in this book will challenge and encourage you to make the most of the moments that you have on this earth.

As I was writing the pages you are about to read, I discovered a song by Mark Harris entitled "Find Your Wings" that made a huge impact on me as a husband and father. While the song is written from the perspective of a parent praying hopefully for his or her child, the context applies to any relationship in our lives and the moments we share. I especially encourage you to reflect on these words from this song as you read this book:

> "May passion be the wind
> That leads you through your days
> And may conviction keep you strong
> Guide you on your way
> May there be many moments
> That make your life so sweet
> Oh, but more than memories
>
> I pray that God will fill your heart with dreams
> And that faith gives you the courage
> To dare to do great things!"

You have been given many moments in life... but only so many moments. The choice is up to you. What are you going to do and who are you going to be.... IN THE MOMENT?

Moments

2

A Defining Moment

"When a defining moment comes along, you can do one of two things. Define the moment, or let the moment define you."
- *Tin Cup* (motion picture, 1996), Ron Shelton (Director), Regency Enterprises/Warner Bros. Pictures

Defining moments don't just happen by chance; they occur when preparation, opportunity, and providence collide. Are you defining your moments? Or, are they defining you? Are you reactively existing or proactively living the life you have been given? And, what role do we really play in a defining moment? Can we really script the defining moments like a screenwriter with ultimate authority to compose the perfect climax?

The date was October 9, 2005. The Houston Astros were playing the Atlanta Braves in the National League Division Series playoff game. Here are some key numbers from that day:

- 18 Innings.
- 42 Players.
- 553 Pitches.
- 5 hours 50 minutes.
- **Houston Astros**: 7   **Atlanta Braves**: 6

Houston fans were treated to 2 games for the price of 1 on this particular Sunday as the Astros clinched a victory to advance to the next round of the playoffs in probably the greatest game ever played. There were so many stories from a game this long, but I was especially intrigued by the story of Chris Burke, who hit the game-winning home run in the bottom of the 18th inning.

Chris came into the game in the 10th inning as a pinch runner. As he was standing on second base, he dreamed about what it would be like to score the winning run. He didn't realize, however, that this moment wouldn't occur until 8 innings later and in a much more dramatic way than he could have ever imagined!

With one out in the 18th inning, Chris came up to bat. He had thoughts about bunting his way to first and actually faked a bunt and then pulled his bat back. After another pitch was thrown for a ball, Chris took the swing of his life and hit a rocket into the Crawford boxes in left field for a history-making home run.

I have gotten to know Chris over the last 3 years, and he is a great person and a great player. He is such a gamer and wants to be in these kinds of situations when the game is on the line. I doubt he could have imagined when he woke up Sunday morning and left for Minute Maid Park what would be in store for him and his teammates that day. In his wildest dreams, he could not have scripted a better story in one of the greatest playoff games ever played.

In life, we script small stories based on limited vision. The irony is that we think we are crafting big stories for big stars (i.e. ourselves). It would be easier if you could have total control over the story of your life. You could determine the plot, the climax, the defining moments, the lead actor (you), and the supporting actors (people who give you praise and glory). Consider the following passage from my friend Louie Giglio's book *I Am Not but I Know I AM*:

"It's a place that requires a constant choice. We can choose to cling to starring roles in the little-bitty stories of us, or we can exchange our fleeting moment in the spotlight for a supporting role in the eternally beautiful epic that is the Story of God.

Think of it as trading up. Abandoning the former and embracing the latter will allow our little lives to be filled with the wonder of God as we live for His fame and the unending applause of His name. And joining our small stories to His will give us what we all want most in life anyway: the assurance that our brief moments on earth count for something in a story that never ends."

Our mind cannot conceive what God has in store for us. We are playing in the greatest game – Life. We need to make sure our lives count for what matters most.

After Sunday's game, Chris Burke remembered the question: 'How do you make God laugh?' Answer: 'Tell Him your plans.' Chris was quoted as saying: "You just never know what the story's going to be, where you're going to end up. To get that hit in that setting was a huge thrill, and something I feel blessed to have done." Yes, Chris Burke played a huge part in this game and, ultimately, the history of the Astros. What Chris was also saying is that this moment pales in comparison to the bigger story of which he is playing a supporting role.

Defining a Moment

A defining moment is packaged with purpose and passion. Defining moments help us become clear about our priorities and our direction. They sometimes involve a change in direction or confirmation about which path to pursue. In our lives, we will have at least one defining moment. A moment that transforms us. A moment that defines who we are, where we have been, and where we are going. A moment that creates clarity about our purpose and calling in life. Some of us have several defining moments. The thing about these moments is that we cannot always predict the exact time and date that these moments will occur. We can, however, be prepared for the defining moments in our lives, so we can be fully present in the moment.

A moment of decision. A moment of direction. A moment of determination. A moment of dedication. A moment to shine. A moment to take our game to the next level. An opportunity to make a difference in the life of another person. A moment to serve. An opportunity to grow. A moment to discover the art of the possible. Opportunities and possibilities can shoot up like a bloom through the stony ground of life – to paraphrase a U2 lyric – when you truly realize the power of a defining moment in your life.

Due to a lack of preparation, some people go through defining moments and never even realize it, causing them to lose out on the benefits of the moment. You can prepare for defining moments in your life. In fact, preparation is the key to success in defining your moments. For Chris Burke, he had spent a lifetime preparing for a moment like this. But, how do we prepare for something when we cannot predict when it will happen? In a word, defining moments are all about FOCUS.

Principle 1: Focus on the Moment

The first principle that will allow you to make the most of the moments in your life is: Focus on the Moment. My wife takes incredible pictures. I, on the other hand, rarely get to touch our digital camera. My pictures tend to be blurred and not focused on the central people in the picture. You may wonder how a person can take a picture that is out of focus with all of the technology that is available. Somehow, I manage to accomplish this feat. We do this in life as well. We fail to capture a vision for what our lives can be – what the moments in our lives can become.

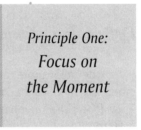

Principle One:
Focus on
the Moment

Focusing on the moment creates clarity and concentration. When you focus on the moment, you gain clarity about what is in front of you – the opportunities, the people involved, the choices, and the decisions you have to make. It is very similar to pressing the focus button on a camera. You press it slightly to put the picture before you into focus. Once you see the objects in front of you clearly in the preview screen, you press the button again to take the picture. And you hope and pray in that split second that nobody blinks or looks another way. The key to focusing on the moment involves discerning what's at stake, who's involved, and how you can make an impact.

The preposition is central to understanding this principle. We all want to be focused and to have focus in the moment. In my research and experience, to have focus *IN* the moment, you must focus *ON* the moment. You have to proactively prepare your heart and mind to be focused. Professional athletes go through a routine to be focused. A business leader reflects on the importance of a key client meeting and considers the questions and advice that will facilitate the best relationship. A high school student practices the conversation in his mind over and over again until he finally musters up the courage to press send on the phone and ask the girl in his science class to the prom.

Focus is fueled by purpose and passion. There must be a point – "a burning Why?" as my friend Spencer Tillman refers to it – to the moments in your life. Consider the following questions to help you focus on the moment:

- Why do you have the platform (i.e. title, role, sphere of influence) that you have?
- What are you doing with that sphere of influence?
- Who is being impacted by your platform?
- How are they being impacted?
- How are you preparing for the defining moments in your life?
- When you think about your entire life as a "moment" in time, how have you prepared yourself to focus on the "moment?"

Preparation begins with an expectancy that your life has meaning and that there is a plan for you life. The following verse from the Bible has provided me comfort throughout my life:

> *"For I know the plans I have for you," declares the LORD, "Plans to prosper you and not to harm you, plans to give you hope and a future. Then you will call upon me and come and pray to me, and I will listen to you. You will seek me and find me when you seek me with all your heart."*
>
> - Jeremiah 29:11-13

When you know that you were created for a purpose and mission and that God has a plan for your life, you are much more likely to anxiously anticipate defining moments in your life. This expectancy and hope fuels your preparation. You know the moments will come, and you want to be ready when they do. So, you take inventory of your gifts, talents, and strengths and work to develop them. You become more awake, alive and fully engaged in life knowing that each moment is leading to something meaningful.

People who are focused on the moment don't wonder if they are making an impact. They are so in tune with the answers to the questions above that the harmony of their lives leaves a legacy for generations to come. As Ken Blanchard reminds us, "The legacy you live is the legacy you leave."

Questions with Answers

Defining moments present you with insightful questions and provide you the opportunity to identify the answers before, during, and after the moment. Specifically, defining moments allow you to answer the following questions:

- Who am I?
- Where have I been?
- Where am I going?

Who am I?

How often do you get a chance to ask that question of yourself? Better yet, how often do you take time out of your busy, sometimes monotonous life and reflect on this very important question? Who am I? Who was I meant to be? Who am I becoming? Do I like the person I am? Was I created to be more than who I am? Sometimes, these questions can feel like a wave crashing in on the shore of our daily routine. We feel overwhelmed by what the answers are or might be, and so we walk away from another opportunity to get in touch with our true self.

These questions are not always deep and philosophical. Many times, they are very practical and pertinent. A moment that defines who we are and who we can become is a very potent and powerful moment. Habits, routines, and ruts can blur the lines of definition around our true self. Defining moments provide clarity and distinction about you – your true character and identity. The picture begins to take form. Objects in the mirror that appeared further away now become closer and clearer into view. Who we are in these moments is the first step to realizing the power of a defining moment. Consider the following questions regarding yourself in a defining moment:

- Am I authentic in all of my relationships?
- Am I expressing myself for who I truly am?
- What am I learning about myself – my character, my personality, my willpower, and my identity?
- Am I being all that I was created to be in the defining moment?
- Am I unleashing all of who I am in the defining moment?
- Am I missing the moments in my life?
- Am I lost during the moments in my life?
- Are defining moments helping me discover my true self?

Where Have I Been?

> *"Cause it seems I get so hung up on,*
> *The history of what's gone wrong.*
> *That the hope of a new day is sometimes hard to see.*
> *But I'm finally catching on to it.*
>
> *Yeah, the past is just a conduit,*
> *And the light there at the end is where I'll be."*
>
> - "Up and Up," song by Relient K

Defining moments provide clarity about the paths we have taken and help us understand the lessons from the past. In "The Road Not Taken," Robert Frost penned a poem about his reflections on the meaning of a defining moment in his past:

> *"Two roads diverged in a yellow wood,*
> *And sorry I could not travel both*
> *And be one traveler, long I stood*
> *And looked down one as far as I could*
> *To where it bent in the undergrowth;*
>
> *I shall be telling this with a sigh*
> *Somewhere ages and ages hence:*
> *Two roads diverged in a wood, and*
> *I took the one less traveled by,*
> *And that has made all the difference."*

When we look in the rearview mirror, do things become cloudy or clear? Fuzzy or focused? Dim or distinct? The past often serves as a prelude of the path to come. In the midst of a defining moment, we discover discernment about whether to continue down the path we are on or to blaze a trail in another direction. Defining moments give us this opportunity. If something in your past has been hindering you from becoming all you can be, a defining moment can provide an opportunity to chart a course correction for your life. Redirection is the key. Redirecting your choices. Redirecting your relationships. Redirecting your responses. Redirecting your course.

Alfred was a very successful chemist, engineer, and businessman who had invented a way to dramatically reduce the cost of blasting rock, drilling tunnels, and building canals. Many mining and construction companies purchased his products. An unintended consequence of his invention was that the military begin to use dynamite for blowing up other armies and towns. Alfred, who was a pacifist and did not support this misuse of his creation, boldly proclaimed:

> *"My dynamite will sooner lead to peace than a thousand world conventions. As soon as men will find that in one instant, whole armies can be utterly destroyed, they surely will abide by golden peace."*

As the military continued to use Alfred's dynamite as a destructive force, a defining moment occurred that forced him to redirect his legacy. The year was 1888, and his brother Ludwig died while staying in Cannes, France. The French newspapers mistakenly reported the death of Alfred, with one headline that read "Le marchand de la mort est mort," translated "The merchant of death is dead."

Alfred Nobel was presented with an opportunity that most of us never receive – a look into the legacy of his life. A case of mistaken identity allowed Alfred to peer into the perception of his legacy. This glance left him speechless. He did not like what he saw, and he vowed to redirect his course if he could. Nobel rewrote his will in 1895 and endowed $9 million to fund what would become known as the Nobel Peace Prize, honoring men and women all over the world for outstanding achievements in physics, chemistry, medicine, literature, and for work in peace. Today, many people associate the name Nobel with peace not war, due to a defining moment in Alfred Nobel's life and an opportunity to make a course correction in his life.

Defining moments can also propel us to a higher level of performance. In these moments, the path we have been traveling is good and has helped prepare us for the moment to come.

Tiger Woods is the best golfer in the game today and maybe of all time. In fact, Jack Nicklaus, admired as the best due to his record of 18 major championship victories, proclaimed, "There isn't a flaw in his golf or his makeup. He will win more majors than Arnold Palmer and I combined. Somebody is going to dust my records. It might as well be Tiger, because he's such a great kid. He has the finest, fundamentally sound golf swing I've ever seen."

In 2007, Tiger won his 13th major golf championship, putting him in striking distance of breaking Nicklaus' record before he finishes his career. His willpower, discipline, and dedication to excellence have been a guiding force in his quest to become his best. With all of the success Tiger has achieved throughout his career, his courage to change and grow has been critical to maintaining his excellence. If someone has success in anything, the tendency is not to mess with success. He or she lives by the mantra, "If it ain't broke, don't fix it." Tiger has lived by a different philosophy striving to perfect his swing for a lifetime. He has modified his swing three times in his career so far, usually after a period of sustained success. Tiger said, "People ask me, 'Are you there yet?' No, you never get there and that's the great thing about it. You can always be better the next day. That's how I look at golf and that's how I look at life. You can always be better."

Tiger Woods has learned how to maintain excellence through the art of redirection – even when his path had been paved with extraordinary achievements and maintaining the status quo would have been the easy choice.

Where Am I Going?

Defining moments drive you to a destination you have never been before. Many times the destination is appealing, similar to the feeling you receive from a stroll on the beach in Maui. Sometimes, however, a defining moment appears appalling.

When I was three years old, my dad divorced my mom. At the time, I did not comprehend what was happening and the fact that this particular moment would be a defining moment in my life. My mom said my immediate concern was for my dad. I asked with the innocence of a child, "Is Dad going to have a place to sleep?" As he came back to our house periodically to take stereo equipment and other household items, I began to wonder if I was going to have a bed to sleep in. At the time, I was not old enough to comprehend the meaning of this moment. All I knew is that I was now different from other kids in my neighborhood and my friends at school, because they had two parents and I did not. Little did I know that this defining moment would affect my direction and the many moments to come in my life. In a positive and powerful way.

For my mom, my dad's sudden departure from our life was a defining moment allowing her to reflect on who she was, where she had been, and where she and this naïve and hopeful little boy were going.

Defining moments help determine your very next step. It is through the defining moment that the next step becomes clear. After gaining clarity about who you are and where you have been, the light shines in the direction you should go. You gain discernment about the meaning of the moment, and the context it provides for the very next moment. As I said before the very next moment could be the very next second or the next 10 years.

One Christmas, we bought a Casio keyboard for one of our boys who is an aspiring musician. The great thing about this keyboard is that it teaches you the notes of certain songs by "lighting up" the appropriate keys to play. As you play a note, the next key displays a red light exclaiming "Play me next!" For a 6-year old aspiring musician or a "wannabe who will never be" musical artist like myself, it becomes very clear what steps to take next. We gain this same clarity when we fully experience a defining moment in our lives. The steps along the path of life become clear, and the paths of roads not taken seem to make sense.

Just Call Me Tom

Blake had just finished the race of his life, competing with his sister for a prize of one million dollars. They lost the race by four minutes. As he pondered the magnitude of the moment, he reflected on what his future would hold. It is not every day that you come so close to winning such a grand prize. He decided that he would take some time to consider his future and left for Argentina.

While he was visiting the country and seeing the needs of the local people, he noticed a pair of shoes that the workers wore in fulfilling their daily jobs. These shoes were not the flashiest or latest style, but he considered them functional and cool. He also noticed that there were many kids who did not have shoes. As he pondered his thoughts underneath the Argentine sky, an idea was birthed that would transform his life. What if a company could sell shoes and give away shoes all at the same time? What if a company could impact the world one child at a time? Blake experienced a defining moment and said to himself, "I'm going to start a shoe company, and for every pair I sell, I'm going to give one pair to a child in need." Not a percentage of profits. Not one shoe for every 20 sold. His epiphany was a one-to-one relationship – one shoe given away for every one shoe sold.

Now, Blake was not just an idealistic philanthropist who did not understand the intricacies of profit and loss. He started his first business at an early age and understood the principles of making a profit. In fact, Blake had run four businesses throughout his twenties and was now approaching thirty with what he thought was his best business idea yet.

Blake had been wearing the "alpargatas" – the shoes that the Argentine workers wore – and liked the feel of the shoe. The shoes were basic, lightweight slip-on shoes that were sturdy enough to take a hike in, but breathable and flexible as well. They had a canvas top and a soft leather insole. Blake began to meet with shoe and fabric makers in Argentina to gain insight and ideas for how to make his idea a reality. He modeled the final product based on the "alpargata" design but made his shoe more colorful with different materials.

An idea was born and a company was created – Toms Shoes, which stands for "Shoes for Tomorrow." The funny thing was that Blake Mycoskie had never worked in fashion. Yet, he was an entrepreneur with a heart for service, and he wanted to make an impact in the lives of others. He was being pulled and propelled by a calling higher than himself.

P^2: Passion Aligned With Purpose

With a staff of seven full-time employees, six salespeople, and eight interns, Toms Shoes developed a line of 15 different styles by June of 2006. Along the way, Blake asked his sister and her friends about where they could distribute their shoes. With some amount of skepticism, they playfully gave him a list of some of the most exclusive shops in the greater Los Angeles area. They did not really expect him to have much success actually convincing these stores to let a $38 pair of canvas slip-on shoes sit side-by-side with a $400 pair of shoes. Yet, this Texan persevered and spoke with passion about his purpose of making a difference in the lives of children all over the world through the mission of Toms Shoes. It was not about the shoes, and, yet, all about the shoes.

"It's all about passion!" Blake emphatically said. "If a storeowner is responsible for buying shoes that they think other people are going to buy, that can be a pretty mundane job, even if they see the latest fashion in shoes. At the end of the day, they are still a merchant. Everyone wants to be around something they believe in and serves the greater good – believer or non-believer. When I go in there and I am so passionate about helping people and also getting the shoe out there, the barrier for them to say 'No' to me was probably less than had I just been trying to sell regular shoes. They saw that the motivation wasn't just financial for me, but it was a large part in helping people."

By the Fall of 2006, Toms Shoes had sold 10,000 pair of shoes and were being sold in places such as American Rag and Fred Segal in Los Angeles and Scoop in New York City as well as through the Toms web site. Staying true to his promise, Blake took a team to Argentina and made their first shoe drop in October, 2006. Blake and his team of a dozen volunteers including his sister gave away 10,000 pair of shoes to needy children across 2,200 miles throughout the Argentina countryside.

Blake points to this moment – his company's first shoe drop – as the real defining moment of his life. "A defining moment was when we did our first shoe drop in Argentina in October," Blake revealed. "The idea for Toms came when I personally experienced seeing kids without shoes and wanting to help them. But it wasn't until I actually took a group of volunteers and my parents and my brother and my sister to Argentina and actually put the shoes on their feet. That moment when the first group of a hundred kids were lining up to get the first pair of shoes on their feet and seeing my sister put shoes on children's feet or looking over and seeing one of my original interns putting shoes on children's feet. That was a very emotional and defining moment in my life. It was a moment where I realized I am no longer an entrepreneur, but this is my life calling.

"The word *entrepreneur* was a good word to describe me prior to Toms, because an entrepreneur starts a business with the idea of selling it and then moving on and starting another business. Now, I have no desire to move on. I feel like I have found my perfect situation – my calling – and there's millions of people who need shoes. At that moment, I knew I was in the right place at the right time. I feel so blessed, because I think there's less than one percent of the world's population who feel like they have found their life's calling and the peace that comes with it. And I feel like I definitely have."

The Bible had definitely impacted Blake at an early age. During his life, he had made a decision to be a follower of Jesus Christ, and there were certain verses that had influenced him, especially when it came to how he was going to run Toms Shoes. Exodus 23:19 says, "Bring the best of the first fruits of your soil to the house of the LORD your God." Romans 7:4 states, "So, my brothers, you also died to the law through the body of Christ that you might belong to another, to Him who was raised from the dead, in order that we might bear fruit to God." He was putting these verses into practice, but it wasn't an easy journey.

After selling his first 10,000 pairs of shoes, colleagues and friends advised him not to make the shoe drop. They told him to wait another year and start making some money before you give the shoes away. Sound business advice, but Blake had made a commitment and a promise. Blake said, "At the time, we were losing money pretty heavily every month. But, we said for every pair of shoes we sell, we are going to give one pair away, and we didn't want to let more than 6 to 8 months go by from the time people bought them until the time the kids received them. When we returned from the first shoe drop, we were overwhelmingly blessed from orders from Nordstroms, Bloomingdales, and Urban Outfitters – big, big stores that some companies would spend years trying to get into. For me, it has been a way of actually seeing scripture come to life in a way that was a lot more meaningful than a lot of my other 'Christian' experiences throughout my life."

Blake was experiencing a clarity he had never seen before. Defining moments do this. They provide clarity and definition to situations and moments that seemingly once appeared as a black hole. Defining moments reveal a distinction between courage and compromise. We are either going to be courageous in the moment or follow a path of compromise.

As Blake reflected on his life journey, he said, "I was really blessed with the ability to be an entrepreneur and get things done and raise money and start new businesses at a very young age – I started my first company when I was eighteen – but it really wasn't until I had an idea about a company that would truly be giving back and helping people as its number one criteria for being in business. With Toms Shoes, I feel like God has really blessed me. I've started some businesses. I have had some success. I have had some failures. But, I hadn't really had something that really, really took off like Toms has."

Faith Provides the Fuel

Matthew 6:33 promises, "But seek first His kingdom and His righteousness, and all these things will be given to you as well." As the leader and "Chief Shoe Giver" at Toms Shoes, Blake is definitely not seeking his kingdom. He saw a need and has used his entrepreneurial skills to make a difference in the world. Blake has chosen a servant's mentality that permeates every part of Toms Shoes. Imagine that – a business that believes its existence is to serve others – to serve its community locally, regionally, and around the world. Blake has truly been inspired to make his life count and to put his time, talents, and money to their highest and best use. He has also stayed true to his commitment of giving away a pair of shoes for every pair bought, even when there seemed to be an insurmountable cash flow deficit.

It takes a tremendous amount of faith to pursue your calling. Sometimes, you are not sure about the very next step or which direction you should go. When you are in the sweet spot of your calling and you have experienced a defining moment, the clarity and definition you gain provide confidence and reassurance that you are traveling down the right road.

"What is faith?" pondered Blake. "Faith is believing in something that you don't have 100 percent empirical data or proof or that you can see or touch. Faith is exactly what I have to exhibit every day when I am building the Toms business. We are a small company. We do literally live month to month based on what comes in. I have faith that we are going to continue to sell 60 pairs of shoes a day online, but there's no promise of that. There's no guarantee. We don't have a formula or advertising campaign that we know will continue to bring us business. We have faith that God will continue to bring us customers and that people will continue to tell their friends. A lot of what I do every day in running the business is having faith that if I am doing what the right thing is, that I will continue to be provided for."

Upon reflection over the last year and Blake's journey with Toms, two themes have become abundantly clear to him. First, you don't need a lot of material things to be happy and have true joy in your life. Blake explained, "The awareness that people in certain parts of the world have so little will naturally drive you to not seek material things. Relationships. Friendships. A great network people that want to help you. That's where I really derive a lot of joy. The second theme that has become abundantly clear is that if you are doing something to help people, other people will help you do it. If you are really pure in your motivation, it is amazing the type of people that will go above and beyond with no compensation – totally selflessly – to help you out."

Through defining moments, Blake has found his true calling and is discovering the heart of a servant leader. You can be truly blessed and rewarded for helping others, and the blessing comes in the serving. "You have to recognize that life is really made up of moments," shared Blake. "The most important thing is to recognize and relish the present. Don't always be looking forward to the next thing or lamenting in the past. Life is made of moments. When you do have one of those moments, take time to recognize it, relish in it, and hopefully remember and store it, because it may be awhile before you have another one."

In November, 2007, Blake Mycoskie and a team of passionate people with a heart for service delivered 50,000 shoes to children in South Africa. I am reminded of the quote that says:

> *"To the world, you may be one person; but to one person, you may be the world."*
> -   Anonymous

Blake and his team have discovered a way to make an impact one person at a time, and their influence is having a significant impact on a lot of children and people with needs.

The Truth about Defining Moments

Here are some simple truths about defining moments:

- Defining moments can be big or small.
- The meaning and significance of defining moments can be realized before, during, and/or after the moment.
- Defining moments create an environment to discover new possibilities, which help open your eyes to reveal exciting opportunities.
- A defining moment is something that you have never experienced before and you are never, ever the same.

- Defining moments steer you in new directions and provide opportunities for charting and correcting your course.
- Defining moments shape and mold your life and your character.
- Defining moments provide clarity and confirmation about direction and purpose.
- Preparation and focus are paramount to discovering and experiencing defining moments.

3

A Missing Moment

"Honey, have you seen the keys?"
  - A husband every day in America

Is the moment missing, or did you miss the moment? Are we looking for something that has become misplaced, or are we truly missing something that can never be replaced? A moment in time is something to be cherished, honored, and anticipated. We foolishly believe that we have all the time in the world, that moments are in full supply, and that we can regain moments that we have missed. We treat missing moments like something that has been lost, anxiously looking around as if we were trying to discover where we placed the keys to our car. We ignorantly utter phrases such as:

- "I am going to work a lot while my children are young, so I will have more time with them when they are older."
- "If I only had more time in my day, I could spend more time with my friends and family."
- "I don't have enough time in my day to do the things I really want to be doing."
- "I didn't have time to call you this week."

As my wife often reminds me, it is not that we didn't have time to do something; we chose not to do something. We made a choice about time that took us away from accomplishing a task. Sometimes, these choices are the right choices. Other times they are not. My son Grant helped illuminate this concept for me when he was 3. I had just arrived home from an out-of-town speaking engagement, and Grant asked if we could play catch. He had a baseball in one hand and a glove in the other and was anticipating a great moment with Dad. I replied, "OK, let me take a quick look at the mail, and then we can play catch together." A minute or two passed while I looked quickly at the mail. After glancing at a few bills and noting the cover story of the latest issue of Sports Illustrated, I turned to discover that Grant was nowhere to be found. The only thing I saw was a handless glove and a baseball in the spot where he once stood. I searched anxiously for him and found him outside riding his bike with his brothers. When I told him that I was now ready to play baseball with him, he responded, "No, I am riding my bike now." Grant had moved on to the next moment. A moment in time, albeit just a minute or two, had passed, and I had missed it!

Based on your purpose, priorities, and passions, are you making the right choices about the time that you have in a day, a week, a year, or your lifetime? What filter are you using to schedule your priorities? Does your calendar run you, or do you run your calendar?

I recently had a conversation with a friend where he was lamenting the fact that he did not have more time in his day to spend with his family, his friends, and the people who matter most to him. He was also frustrated that he was not attending to the right priorities in his life, both at work and at home. His victim mindset was hindering him from uncovering the secrets to missing moments. I finally interrupted his monologue and challenged him by saying, "The moments are not missing; you missed them. They were right there in front of you, and you chose not to see them." Are the moments missing in your life like keys that you cannot find, or are you missing the moments like ships passing before you in the night?

"To be or not to be; that is the question."
- from the play "Hamlet," William Shakespeare

While this quote was originally framed in the context of pondering death versus life, every day many people pose this question as life versus life: "To engage or not to engage; that is the question." To be fully there or not fully there. To live life to the fullest or to live life to the least. To be intentional with my life or let life pass me by. However you want to phrase this question, we all struggle with this at some point in our lives.

While you may know people who are not fully there, I am talking about focus, not faculties. Many times, the focus is there in one aspect of their life like work or a fitness program. The sad part is that focus in other areas of their life is lacking. They are not a whole person living a whole life for a whole lifetime. They choose not to engage either by design or by default and lose out on all that life can be for them and for those around them. As Alvah Simon said so prophetically in his book *North to the Night*, "Death is only one of many ways to lose your life."

One of my most embarrassing moments happened when I was a freshman in high school. It was not surviving the struggles of being a freshman, but a specific event that highlights my point about engagement in life. I was on the freshman basketball team and didn't play much that particular year. The rest of my high school basketball career was filled with more minutes as I made the varsity team and played for a state championship. Yet, my freshman year was filled with some disappointment. During one particular game, the coach called me to check in, or at least I thought I was checking in. He yelled toward the end of the bench, "Van Hoozer! Get down here! I have a special assignment for you." Now, the thought of a "special assignment" conjured up many meanings for me. Number 20 on the other team had been scoring a lot of points against us, and I thought our coach wanted me to shut him down.

Another image I had was of me scoring the winning basket. I thought they were finally going to call my number and run a "special" play just for me. Evidently, our coach had a different definition of the word *special*.

As I jumped from my seat on the bench and approached him, our coach revealed the special assignment. He looked at me with all the seriousness of a secret agent and said, "Mike, our scoreboard has been shorting out, and I need you to go down to the scorer's table and hold the plug into the floor socket for the rest of the game." This was not the special assignment I had in mind. I don't recall what I said to him after that. Maybe, I said something like, "Yes Sir, Coach!" "Got it, Coach!" "I won't let you down, Coach!" I do, however, know what I was thinking. My first thought was maybe this was my chance to prove I could handle the smaller things like a scoreboard short-out, so I could eventually get into the game. This was not the typical route to getting some playing time in a game. Typically, you practice hard, demonstrate your potential and ability, which results in playing time. This circuitous route to getting into a game seemed odd, but I resolved myself to do my best. So for the rest of the game, I sat in front of the scorer's table holding the plug in the socket in the floor. With excellence!

Now my next thought was about how I was going to explain this to my family and friends. I began to realize that this was becoming a very embarrassing moment. I began to think about this moment and wonder how many people might witness the event. You see, not a lot of fans attend freshman basketball games. The games are usually right after school, while the varsity game is reserved for prime time and a bigger audience. We did, however, have a lot of students, like the seniors, come through the gym after football practice. Sometimes, they would stop and watch, not because they were interested in the freshman team, but because they might catch some hilarious play to make fun of the next day at school. I looked around the gym. It seemed like an inordinate amount of newfound "fans" were gathering at one end of the gym. I began to think of how embarrassing this moment was going to be. How was I going to explain this? This moment would provide fodder for tomorrow's locker room and hallway conversations.

- "Did you see the player who did not check into the game yesterday?"
- "Yeah, I think he was playing around with the scoreboard?"
- "Is he even on the team?"

My mind became a whirlwind. As I was pondering my explanation for tomorrow, the moment of truth happened. The ball went out of bounds, the referee blew his whistle, and time stood still. The referee, thinking I was waiting to check in, motioned for me to come into the game. My heart was beating profusely, and I did not want to get into a long, drawn out explanation of why I was sitting at the scorer's table seemingly playing with the scoreboard plug. So, I very calmly motioned to him and said in the coolest voice I could muster something like "No, I'm good." The referee, agitated that this freshman did not get it, sternly said, "No, son, you don't understand. This is the time when you check into the game!" At this point, I humbly explained that I was just sitting on the side holding the plug to the scoreboard. I may have expounded on the thought of how I believed that this special assignment was one day going to get me into the game. As the referee said, "OK," they quickly resumed the game. I sat there for the final moments just watching from the sideline. I was oblivious to any laughter or humiliation that I might face the next day. The only thought that echoed in my head was: "I am sitting here and wearing the uniform; yet, I am not checking in."

So is life for some people. They are wearing the uniform but not checking in – just sitting on the side watching life go by. The disturbing part is that these same people who are not checking in think they are very much in the game. This delusional thinking is demonstrated in many ways. A father incessantly pounding away at his blackberry, oblivious to the fact that his daughter just scored the winning basket. A leader passively standing by while integrity is forsaken. A spouse serving leftovers at the end of a hard day's work to the people who matter most. A student waiting for a future moment to be purposeful, wasting precious moments that cannot be regained. They think they are participants, not realizing they are just merely spectators.

All the while, a chorus rises up around them with the same resounding theme: "CHECK IN to the GAME of LIFE! Your teammates NEED YOU!"

What is Your Deepest Fear??

In the movie Coach Carter, actor Samuel L. Jackson plays a basketball coach who challenges his players to be more than athletes and to strive for excellence in everything they do including their schoolwork. This movie is a true story about Ken Carter and his Richmond High School basketball team. Throughout the movie, he asks a very probing question of one of his players:

> *"What is your deepest fear?"*

For some people, this question represents a conflict with the very essence of who they are. They have been created for a calling but have failed to answer the phone. Fear keeps them from answering the ring of responsibility. We most often associate this fear with failure, but many times the fear that locks in your potential is a deep, hidden fear of success. In my work with high performance athletes, I see this fear of success rear its ugly head and keep them from reaching the next level of achievement. The problem is uncovering this hidden secret, because nobody wants to admit that they have a fear of success.

Everyone wants to be successful, achieve goals, and perform at their best. The fear of success comes into play when a player begins to think about the consequences of success. They realize that success is a double-sided coin, and on the other side lies failure. To take a chance on performing successfully in the moment, you have to be willing to deal with the risk of failure. The following model illustrates the stages of the fear of success.

Figure 3.1 - Fear of Success Model.

Fear

The first stage is a base level of fear. You cannot discern what the fear is, but you absolutely sense it. It is real and apparent in your life. You try and repress it, but it keeps surfacing similar to the struggle you have when you try and keep a beach ball under water in the pool. The harder you attempt to hold it under the water, the higher the beach ball jumps into the air once it escapes the grasp of your hands. So it is with fear. Fear cannot be repressed, but it can be replaced. Olympic athletes teach us how to combat our fears and replace the thoughts that so often hinder us. The Olympic games happen once every four years. Athletes who compete for the privilege of representing their country in these elite games experience a tremendous amount of pressure to perform. Typically, these athletes have one shot at an event called the Olympic trials to qualify to compete in the Olympic games later that same year. If they don't perform on that day, they have to wait another four laborious years. Some people would try to repress these thoughts of fear and pressure and not think about them. Successful Olympians replace thoughts of fear and obstacles with thoughts of faith and possibilities. Acknowledging the pressure and putting those thoughts on the table are the best way to combat your fears and replace them with better thoughts.

Uncertainty

The next stage is uncertainty. You begin to consider a stage beyond your fears, but you become uncertain about what that might look like. You begin to consider possibilities, but the fuzziness of the future derails you from taking the first step to success. It seems safer to stay on the shore than to jump in the current of life.

Doubt

For those of you brave enough to dip your toe into the water, doubt is there to meet you head on. Doubts about yourself, your abilities, your talents, and your strengths. Voices around you and within you begin to join in a chorus that commands you to go back to the shore. They begin to replay every time you have tried and failed. Your voice begins to rise above the choir of doubt and sing a solo that convinces yourself to stay where you are.

Identity

While the song of doubt sounds convincing, you persevere covering your ears to move to the next stage of identity. At this stage, you consider your identity. Does your identity remain a question? People who get locked into this stage never seem to discover who they are, why they are here, and what they are to do? This stage can be paralyzing or propelling depending on the answer to the question of who you are.

Risk

Once you have discovered who you are, you face the stage of risk. You come to grips with the reality of what is before you. To become all of who you are and do all that you have been called to do will require risks.

Most people are risk averse. You can never realize your full potential without some level of risk. The key question remains: Is it really "risky" to pursue who you were designed to be?

Expectations

The final stage up the mountain of fear is expectations. You begin to consider the possibility of success, envision what that would look like, and fear that the expectations will be too great for you to deal with. You think that raising your game will raise the expectation level of those around you, and you convince yourself that the level you are at is much more comfortable and safe. You have reached a level of success, you know what that looks and feels like, and you don't want to cross over the mountain for fear you cannot meet the expectations that it might require.

The Other Side of the Mountain

There is another side of the mountain of the fear of success. It can propel you to new heights if you are willing to venture to the other side. Do you want to take a look?

Figure 3.2 Fear of Success Model - the other side of fear.

Encouragement

Once you venture to the other side of the mountain, you immediately begin to receive encouragement. Friends and family begin to recognize and recall innate gifts and talents that you have. They sing a song of support that alleviates your fears and quiets the voice of unattainable expectations. They provide encouragement about your strengths, gifts, and talents and help you identify aspects of your life that you didn't even realize existed. You begin to join in this chorus and begin to realize that there is a plan for your life and that you have the tools to execute this plan. You have been wired a certain way for a certain purpose. The results will be revealed to you on a daily basis as you live your life for what matters most.

Results

The next stage is where you begin to experience results from your efforts. As you step out in faith, you realize that you are achieving success, accomplishing goals, and fulfilling your life purpose. Moreover, you see the impact and influence that living your life to the fullest can have on the people in your story. Positive results come in many forms. For an athlete, it could be a big tournament win or a feeling of knowing that you did your absolute best. For a businessperson, results could come in the form of a big sale or helping someone achieve their goals and develop in their career. For a parent, it could surface as becoming fully engaged in the development of your son or daughter's life. For a spouse, it could be finally providing a listening ear. Whatever the format, positive results provide the best feedback that you are on the right track.

Reinforcement

Once you have achieved results, reinforcement is the best way to maintain momentum in your life. Achieving excellence in your life is one thing; maintaining excellence is even harder. Reinforcement is the best way to help you maintain a new level of excellence and accomplishment in your life. In this stage, you achieve additional results and with that comes additional encouragement. You begin to prove to yourself and others that the success you had in the last stage was not just a fluke. Again, think in terms of every area of your life. Not only do you go 2-4 in the baseball game last night, you experience those kinds of results for a week or a month. You demonstrate to your wife that you can be understanding and empathetic more than once in a lifetime, even while the "big football game" is beckoning for your attention. You prove to your son that you can make more than one practice or game in his little league career – without your blackberry attached to your hip. You communicate to your people that you believe in them, and they really trust you this time, because you have shown this on more than one occasion. Whatever the area of your life, you maintain a new level of excellence that is reinforced by your behaviors and the encouragement you receive from others about your sustained level of performance. People begin to say things like:

- "Wow, you sure have changed! And for the better, I might add!"
- "I have really noticed you helping around the house, and I wanted you to know how much I appreciate it."
- "You are really in a groove right now."
- "Keep up the great work."
- "You are playing in the zone."
- "I'm proud of you!"

Additional encouragement and repeated results are the key factors to momentum in this stage.

Impact

Once you experience the reinforcement stage, you begin to look outside yourself and discover the impact that you are having on people around you. It begins with your friends and family. Your new level of performance provides support and encouragement for them to perform at their best. It encourages them to take risks and pursue their maximum potential. They gain inspiration from your story and are challenged to discover how they should play the part in their own story. Also, when you do your best, it always makes your teammates and your organization better. This concept is true whether we are talking about a family organization, a business, a church, a non-profit group, or a sports team. A team comes together when individuals rally around a cause and truly play the parts they are given. Life is not just all about you. Life is relational. We have been created as relational beings, and you were created to have an impact on the lives of other people.

Confidence

The stage of confidence is reached as you begin to experience the momentum of all that has preceded this moment. You think about the uphill struggle of the left-hand side of the mountain. You consider what you have overcome – fear, uncertainty, and doubt. You realize who you are including your purpose and your calling. You acknowledge the way you have stepped out in faith and avoided the trap of expectations to reach the other side of the mountain. Once there, you have received encouragement, positive results, reinforcement, and you have impacted and influenced others in the best way possible. The key factor in reaching this stage is that you have replaced the negative forces of the left-hand side of the mountain with thoughts and experiences on the right-hand side of the mountain. The confidence that you now possess is not an arrogance, but an inherit belief that you have been given a mission and you are pursuing that for a lifetime.

Courage

The final stage is courage. It is very appropriate that this stage parallels fear on the other side of the mountain. Mark Twain said, "Courage is resistance to fear, mastery of fear, not absence of fear." Fear cannot be repressed, but the thought of fear that so tightly binds us can be replaced by thoughts of confidence and courage to help give us the ability to overcome our fear. Courage begins with encouragement. In fact, the words courage and encouragement are derived from the Latin word "cor," meaning "heart." Encouragement literally means to give heart to another person. Thus, the idea that we have courage to conquer our fears commands us to begin this cycle again in the life of another person. Once we possess courage, we must release it for the benefit of other people.

Living in Hi-Def

I saw a commercial the other day that was advertising the amazing picture quality and clarity of a high definition television. The commercial began with a golfer hitting a shot into the rough off of the fairway. The next shot showed fans watching the golf tournament from their high definition television. The people at home could see exactly where the ball had landed, but the golfer could not find it. As the golfer and a team of people on the golf course aimlessly searched for the ball in the tall blades of grass, the fans watching at home stood up and began to point to the ball, powerlessly trying to help the golfer find his ball. They questioned why he could not see it. The ball was beside him, but the lack of clarity could not allow him to find it.

I began to think about what living a life in high definition would look like. A life in Hi-Def begins with identifying and connecting with your purpose. Why are you here? How did you get here? Why now – in this moment – are you here? Who were you created to be, and what were you created to do? Purpose answers all of these questions.

The second major aspect of living a life in Hi-Def involves passion. Do you love who you are? Do you love what you are doing? Not just in one area of your life, like work, but in all areas of your life. Does getting out of the bed, even on Monday morning, fire you up? Do your eyes light up when you think about the opportunity to live another day? Passion is the pilot light that ignites our purpose. In fact, the new math of our lives should be:

P^2 = Passion and Purpose – the ideal formula for living a life in Hi-Def

You do not have to go out and buy a new television to experience a life of high definition. You can discover this clarity by escaping the clutter and noise from your life and making the time to ponder the questions of purpose and passion in your life. For me, living in Hi-Def clarity has been found through my faith, my family, my friends, and my role. First, my faith in God and Jesus Christ has helped me discern the reason I was created and provided me freedom to pursue it passionately for a lifetime. My faith is the foundation for all of who I am and all that I do.

Next, my family provides me incredible clarity about what is most important to me. For many people, it takes a crisis to remind them about what is really important and what they only pretend to care about. I strive each day to give the best to my wife and five boys each day. We make it a priority to make the most of every moment that we have. Are we perfect as a family? No! Do we have missing moments in our lives? Absolutely! Do we mope over these moments? No! We move along. We make the most of the next moment.

I have been blessed to have some incredible friends and mentors in my life. Some made an impact in the moment – a season of my life. Some have continued to influence me to this day. We all need friends, mentors, and wise counselors in our lives. People that know us well enough to encourage, embolden, and energize us to be our best. Confidants that we can be vulnerable with and who are willing to speak the truth in love to us even when it hurts. We accept this truth, because we know they truly care about us and want to build us up, not tear us down. I wholeheartedly believe that the people who are in my life are there for a reason. I didn't just happen to meet them by coincidence. The truth is that you have people in your life that can provide this kind of encouragement and help you discover clarity in your life as well. Do you know who those people are? Are you reaching out to them during both significant and challenging moments in your life?

Finally, my role in life reinforces to me why I am here on a moment-by-moment basis. I am using the term "role" to refer to what is typically called "a job" or "work," which carry connotations of having to do something that I don't necessarily want to do or like to do. Nobody likes to work! Why do you think a lot of people dread Monday mornings? When you find a role, however, that you are truly passionate about, you can't wait for Monday morning. You love what you do, and you believe it was what you were created to do. This role becomes your platform and sphere of influence to accomplish a greater purpose and live a life of value, meaning, and impact.

Don't Miss the Moment

Moments that have been missed are not missing, they are gone! The best we can do is learn from the moment that has been lost, be fully present in the current, and prepare for the next moment to come. The great basketball coach of UCLA and mentor of men John Wooden constantly impressed upon his players the following point:

> *"Make each day your masterpiece."*

Coach Wooden further explained that "the past is gone and will never change, and the future is only impacted by what you do today." In my work with athletes, we constantly emphasize this point. I have worked with very successful and talented baseball players who struggle in a moment, because they are still obsessing over the previous moment – a moment that is dead and gone. They think about the last at bat where they struck out with the bases loaded instead of driving in several runs to help the team. In the next inning, they are in the field physically, but mentally they may not be completely there to focus on the next play. The challenge is to put missing moments behind them, so they can fully perform in the current moment. The rest of this book will focus on techniques that you can use to be fully present during the moments of your life.

Toward the end of the movie *Coach Carter*, Timo Cruz – the player that has been challenged to consider his deepest fear – recites an inspiring passage from the book *A Return to Love* by Marianne Williamson:

> *"Our deepest fear is not that we are inadequate.*
> *Our deepest fear is that we are powerful beyond measure.*
> *It is our Light, not our Darkness, that most frightens us.*
> *We ask ourselves, who am I to be brilliant, gorgeous, talented, fabulous?*
> *Actually, who are you not to be?*
> *You are a child of God. Your playing small does not serve the World.*
> *There is nothing enlightening about shrinking*
> *so that other people won't feel unsure around you.*
> *We were born to make manifest the glory of God that is within us.*
> *It is not just in some of us; it is in everyone.*
> *As we let our own Light shine,*
> *we consciously give other people permission to do the same.*
> *As we are liberated from our own fear,*
> *our presence automatically liberates others."*

We can never do anything about missing a moment. We can never change yesterday; we can, however do something about today that will also impact tomorrow. What are you doing to improve your today and impact your tomorrow? Your life is here and now. Don't miss the moment!

4

A Disappearing Moment

"On a day like this I want to crawl beneath a rock
A million miles from the world, the noise, the commotion
That never seems to stop."
 - from the song "Disappear" by Bebo Norman

Do you ever feel like this? You just want to crawl beneath a rock and never come out. Or, maybe, you do want to emerge at some point; but for right now, you are content to hibernate in a hole. The commotion and the noise are clamoring around you, contending for your every last bit of undivided attention. Some things important. Others urgent. Some inconsequential. Deciphering this mess can require a level of clarity many people never possess. Or, they don't take the time to possess it. The key question is do we disappear in the moment?

"Sr." was a high-school standout in basketball. He played point guard and was the captain of his team on the floor. He showed up every night and played his heart out. His skills and efforts helped him make the all-city team and paved the way for him to play college basketball.

During this time, a friend set him up on a blind date with a cheerleader from a rival high school. Eventually, they got married, bought a house, and had a son. "Jr." became destined to follow in the footsteps of his father's awesome accomplishments. They also became pregnant with another child who was lost along the way. Little did they realize at the time that they would eventually lose much more than an unborn child.

Jr. began to grow and develop in the usual way. Early pictures showed him with all kinds of balls, but his favorite ball was a basketball. At the age of 18 months, he could dribble a ball twice the size of his face all over the house. He experienced all of the normal events that occupy a child's life. Walking by the age of 10 months. Wearing cake all over his face for his first birthday. Playing peek-a-boo for hours with his parents and with strangers who he was yet to know. While Jr. loved playing this magic act, he was about to witness a disappearing act that would have a profound effect on the rest of his life and the life of his parents. Sr. was on the verge of a magic trick that would far surpass the naïve nature of a simple game of peek-a-boo.

As Jr. grew up, his parents grew apart. Or, better said, his father grew apart. The child who never came – a daughter and sister – was only a symptom of a deeper issue. Jr.'s mother was sick every single day of her pregnancy with his sister. What Jr. did not know was that the nausea associated with the pregnancy would pale in comparison to the grief that was to come. Jr. also was too young to comprehend the catastrophe that was brewing inside the four walls of a house they once called home. Jr.'s father was becoming a master magician, leading a double life with mirrors, curtains, and a façade of false character.

Sr. began hanging with a "fast" crowd. "Fast" games of tennis followed by infidelity and divorce. Work was no better at providing an environment that supported the sanctity of a sacred union between a man and a woman. Everyone else was doing whatever he or she wanted to do. If it felt good, they did it without any consideration for the consequences. Sr. followed the crowd, disappearing behind the curtain of deceit and duplicity. Only two people were in the audience of this tragic magic act, left wondering, "Where did he go?"

I was 3 and a half when this disappearing act happened. My father walked out on my mother and disappeared from our lives. My mom held out hope that he would return – that the disappearing act was not for real. The magician usually reappears from behind the curtain after the final trick to take a bow and receive the applause. She could not conceive why the curtain was not moving. There was no applause to be found. She prayed about the alternatives. Divorce was definitely not in her vocabulary. After a year and a half of Sr. defiantly declaring that he was not coming back, she found peace about the "D" word, or better said, learned to live with it as an inevitable reality. Through the counsel and reassurance of friends, family, and her faith in God, she proceeded to go along with the process of bringing this act to its climax.

What happens when the magic act is not just an illusion? What happens when you peel back your hands from your eyes and he is no longer there? Surely, he is coming back. In moments like these, the cries of "This can't be happening!" turn into "Why did this happen?" Feelings of failure, regret, disappointment, disillusionment, and powerlessness engulf your emotions and your mind. What do you do when the person you were counting on the most just up and disappears, leaving a puff of smoke and a trail of what ifs along the way.

The Cave or the Comforter?

> *"And on a day like this I want to run away from the routine*
> *Run away from the daily grind that can suck the life*
> *Right out of me*
> *I know of only one place I can run to."*
> - from the song "Disappear" by Bebo Norman

Where do you go? Who do you turn to? My mom had some huge decisions in front of her. How was she going to make it as a single mom?

All of the other mothers on our street got to choose to stay home with their children. She had no choice. At her weakest moments, she desperately pleaded, "Why can't I be home during the day, spending time with my son? Why do I have to work?"

In a matter of moments, she had lost a husband and a baby. There were many moments of frustration where she could not muster up the energy to pray, because every time she began to converse with God, she saw her baby's face. She was not angry and bitter; she just felt severe feelings of hurt and grief. Grief is ten times worse than being sad. She later told me that sadness was what she felt when her parents died after ninety full years of a life well lived. Grief was what she felt at this moment, because a life had been taken, seemingly before its time.

She was young, scared to death, embarrassed, and distraught. In this moment, she turned to family and friends. She shared with her parents that she felt like her son's life was ruined. He would not grow up with a father in the usual way, and she felt responsible, although it was not her fault. Her parents offered open arms of support, love, and encouragement during this time.

She also sought the support and counsel of friends. One friend in particular provided profound advice that would mark a turning point in this desperate situation. It was the kind of advice that transcends the wisdom of human minds. This person was Mary Ann Frazier. Mary Ann was a wife, a mother of 5 boys, and a powerful communicator and teacher at her local church. She taught a Bible study to many people throughout the city. During her lifetime, she had impacted many lives with wisdom from above. Her identity and self-esteem were strong. She knew where her strength and confidence came from, and she was not ashamed to share this with everyone she knew.

My mom had attended her Bible study and truly respected her as a woman of God. My mom referred to her as "the strongest Christian I know." Who better to turn to than a woman like Mary Ann Frazier. As my mom shared with her the despair and grief she felt, Mary Ann listened with an intensity that surpassed human compassion. At the appropriate time in the conversation, Mary Ann empathically said, "Patricia, some people who come to me and share think they have real problems, but you REALLY DO!" Mary Ann comforted my mom and reassured her that everything was going to be all right. She told her that God was in control, and He knew this disappearing act was going to happen before the moment occurred. She went on to say that God had a plan and purpose for her and for her 5-year old son, despite the choices that her husband had made. "Although we may not always know why, everything happens for a reason!" she proclaimed.

Now if Mary Ann had stopped right there and sent her on her way, my mom may have felt better, but she would have still been lacking the knowledge of what to do next. My mom was at a crossroads with real problems and needed real, practical advice on what to do next. Mary Ann's last piece of advice was profound and left an indelible mark for years to come. She said, "Patricia, I want you to go home and pray this prayer:

'God, I pray that you be a father to the fatherless for my son. I also pray that you would provide people in my little boy's life that would step into the place left barren by his biological father.'"

Mary Ann further explained, "This prayer can be found in Psalm 68:5. Patricia, go home, pray this prayer, and claim this truth on a daily basis."

My mom thought about all of the words and the feelings that Mary Ann shared with her. She walked away still wondering about what the future would hold but reassured that someone was watching over her. She went home and read Psalm 68:5:

"*A father to the fatherless, a defender of widows, is God in His holy dwelling.*"

She pondered the impact and truth of this verse and the words she had received from a strong woman of faith. My mom said to herself, "If this verse is good enough to pray once a day, I am going to pray it ten times a day." And so she did. It became a mantra for everything she did and a cornerstone quote to whomever she came in contact with. When I became old enough to understand, she shared it with me. Moment by moment, I saw the truth of this verse unfold.

Faith of Our Fathers

My grandfather was the first male figure that appeared on the scene. His name was Pat, and he was the father of my mother. He was a man of truth and integrity, living his life in such a way that what he said matched up with how he lived. We had "man-to-man" talks, rides in his car, and rides on his lap. I remember, as well as a 5-year old can remember, looking up into his eyes and wanting to be just like him. He invited me to go with him everywhere. It was the ideal mentoring relationship, where I was experiencing what it was like to be a "real man." It didn't seem weird at the time, but as I look back at it, many fathers, and especially grandfathers, didn't provide the kind of insight and access to their life that Pat did for me.

I was proud of Pat, and he was proud of me. He took me – his only grandson and a fatherless one at that – and lived his life before me. Pat took me to play golf before the days of Tiger Woods and child prodigies. At the time, it was rare for a country club to allow a youngster on the course, because it might slow up the game for others. Pat told the suspicious officials at the club that I was his caddy and ball watcher. He insisted that I ride in the cart so that I could give him advice on shots and help him find his ball. I knew I could help him find his golf balls, but at the time, I wasn't so sure about being a caddy. I didn't know the difference between a fade and a draw, much less what club to use in different situations. At the age of 8, the biggest club in the bag looks like the perfect club to use on every shot. He would also let me hit balls on the course during our rounds together. He provided the kind of instruction that is priceless – because of its content and its intent. He was a true coach in golf and in life with the goal of helping me become all that God intended me to become, regardless of the cards I had been dealt.

We had bathroom moments where he taught me how to shave. I remember watching him get ready for work and shaving with a blade. I asked him one day if I could shave too. Instead of some hurried and nervous reply about the dangers of using a blade and the urgency of his schedule, he replied emphatically, "Sure!" He removed the blade from the steel razor and demonstrated which way to hold the razor. I lathered up with enough shaving cream for 3 men to shave and proceeded to act like a real man who was experiencing a rite of passage. He laughed in amusement at the show before him. This was life! Real life! Not some semblance of an existence, but a connection made head to head and heart to heart.

It was the life that I knew. I never once looked back on the day that my dad disappeared. It was what it was. The people who reappeared from behind the curtain stepped in and played a part I could never repay. Pat had faith. Faith in God. Faith in me. And that faith permeated everything I did and all of who I was becoming. This faith was real and authentic.

The Invisible Coach

"*I don't want to care about earthly things*
Be caught up in all the lies that trick my eyes
They say it's all about me
I'm so tired of it being about me..."
- from the song "Disappear" by Bebo Norman

I called him Coach. His name was Walt Holman – a family man who loved his wife and his daughter. He was also a man of faith who had strong character and deep convictions. He also loved his players. He was the kind of man that would never use the word *love* on the basketball court, but you knew he cared about his players in the way that he coached. In everything he did, it was never about him. He had the kind of humility that allows you to be successful. Strong confidence and high self-esteem mixed with the proper amount of vulnerability.

Coach Holman was my high school basketball coach. I first met him my freshman year. He commanded your respect just by walking in a room. I was determined to play varsity ball, so that I could learn from him. Lessons about basketball and about life. My sophomore year, I made the junior varsity team. I remember the first speech he gave to the varsity and junior varsity team like it was yesterday. Coach Holman said, "Men, last year our record was 6-20. We don't go 6-20. I don't like 6-20. We will never be a 6 and 20 team again. Do you understand?" That said it all. He believed it, and he instilled that belief in me and the other players on the team. My junior year, our record was 33-2, and we played for a state championship earning the State Runner-Up title. Our team was the first to accomplish this feat for our high school. It was a banner year for us. We set many records including a winning streak of 19 straight games.

During the entire year, he stuck to his game plan and inspired a belief in us that propelled us to a purpose beyond ourselves. In spite of our awesome record, we became the underdog team that everyone cheered for. We were not the tallest or most talented team, but we played AS A TEAM. While Coach was very visible in our lives, he became like an invisible glue that held us together. The best coaches do this. They display a kind of selfless disappearance. They appear and become actively involved in leading, and then step back and allow their players to shine. They teach, coach, encourage, inspire, and enable you to do things that you never thought you could do. It is almost as if the coach is performing through the athlete. The great thing about Coach Holman is that he never craved the credit. He never seized the spotlight. Our season was always about a higher purpose and a story where he was not the main character. It was not about him.

Coach Holman made a profound impact in my life. He is a man of integrity who reinforces the power of actions that match up with words. He never strays from the right path. In addition to learning how to run a proper basketball practice, he taught me principles and spiritual truths that I carry with me to this day. I use all of these lessons with my boys and the athletes that I coach. He is someone that I call a friend.

He was even there for me on my wedding day as one of my groomsmen. I can remember preparing to walk out before a large crowd of people taking a step that would mark a significant milestone in my life. Coach was there giving me advice. My nickname in high school was "Tiny Nate," modeled after the great "Tiny Nate" Archibald who played professional basketball in the 70's and 80's. Coach told me, "Tiny, this is a great day in your life. When you walk out there and step up to the altar, just remember the same confidence and coolness you displayed every time you stepped up to the free throw line in high school. Getting through this is just like hitting the game-winning free throws. Go out there and make them." What a great speech, especially for an athlete. Maybe, not the most romantic idea. I doubt my wife was thinking that getting married resembled anything like a basketball game. But, Coach Holman was there, once again, instilling a confidence and belief in me and all that I was becoming. His influence continues to touch people that he will never meet through me and others. An invisible hand that touches the lives of other people is an incredible reality. As Robert Browning said, "A man's reach should exceed his grasp."

John's Transformation

What are you disappearing from and where are you disappearing to? Are there areas of your life where you are not appearing? You may be there in person, but your head and heart are not there. For some people, it is their job. Many people just go to work and collect a paycheck. Is this you? Are you just going through the motions, realizing there is something better for you out there but scared to ask the questions to bring clarity to your life?

Maybe, you are showing up doing a great job with the tasks that are assigned to you but missing the broader story that is going on around you. John was a mid-level manager at a major energy company. He progressed in his career in the usual way taking assignments with different divisions of the company including some that required international travel. He advanced at a quick pace for this particular company and eventually gained more and more responsibility. His advancement was primarily based on his technical expertise and his ability to produce. He came to work, completed his individual tasks, and went home.

When he received his promotion to Manager, he was presented with an organizational chart that diagrammed the lives he was now responsible for. In addition to being in charge of tasks and things, he was now responsible for other people and the interrelationships that life brings our way. It was as if he had been behind a curtain for six years and then suddenly appeared to find an audience waiting for him to make an impact. It was not as if the people had not been there all along. He was sure that he had worked in great teams and interacted with people during his career. But, now, it was different. He and the other people were no longer just doing their respective jobs. He felt a sudden responsibility to do something more. It was the same feeling he had after the birth of his first daughter. A life waiting to experience all that life has and counting on the people around her to show her the way.

John began to rethink his role at work and developed a plan for making an impact in the lives of other people. He considered his purpose in life and developed a mission statement that was broad enough to cover all areas of his life – work, family, friends, faith, and community. He began to make his presence known. Not in a braggadocios way like some leaders do exclaiming, "I'm the BOSS!" He began to develop a seemingly counter-leader and counter-culture mentality. His mission statement reflected his newfound actions:

"To lead a life of service by making an impact in the lives of other people."

This statement served as a filter for who he was and what he did. It became a part of his character and his actions. People began to notice the change and feel the impact. He was amazed at the results. At work, not only was he getting things done, he was able to accomplish even more through the efforts of his people. He had always assumed that time away from a task was unproductive. People were a necessary evil, and he only transacted with them to the degree that it helped him get the job done. He never considered the broader picture of how investing in the development of another person was a win-win proposition for him, the other person, and ultimately the organization. His new philosophy inspired him to explain, teach, and help transform the lives of his co-workers. It only took a little bit of time, and the time spent was well worth the return on investment. Tasks were completed, people grew in their careers and assumed more responsibility, and the company was profitable. A perfect cycle of business success!

To date, he had passively considered this principle in his personal life, although his home had become an environment of transactions as well. He and his wife had become ships passing in the night. Soccer practice on Monday night. Cheerleading on Tuesday. Church on Wednesday night. Baseball on Thursday. Their life was becoming a revolving door of activities that kept them from developing their kids in the way that they needed to. It wasn't that any of these activities were bad. It was just that their lives were becoming full of transactions, which were crowding out the time for true transformation. Ultimately, John and his wife were responsible for taking back their so-called life and contending for the time to invest in the character and development of each other and their kids.

John made the change and never looked back. He wrongly assumed that dealing with people would take more time – precious time that he needed to complete "his" tasks. While it did require time, the return on his investment was better than what he had seen on any brokerage statement that came in the mail. He lived by the axiom:

"An ounce of investment is worth a pound of intention."

He became more focused and intentional than any other time in his life. Everyone around felt the impact. His co-workers began to feel more appreciated. His wife felt he was more engaged when he was at home. His kids felt heard and understood. He was present in the moment, he performed in the moment, and he performed beyond the moment. We will explore and unpack these concepts in future chapters.

The Best Disappearing Act

"I want to hide in You
The Way, the Life, the Truth
So I can disappear
And love is all there is to see
Coming out of me
And You become clear
As I disappear."
　　　- from the song "Disappear" by Bebo Norman

Some people don't even know they have the freedom to ask the deeper questions of life:

- Who am I?
- What is my purpose in life?
- Why am I here?
- What is the point of my life?
- Am I making a difference?
- Am I adding value?

You HAVE the freedom to ask the right questions! You must take time to reflect on these questions. You don't want to be like the 2 guys who were taking a road trip without a clue where they were going and having too much manly confidence to ask for directions. The driver eventually said to his clueless passenger, as only one man can say to another, "I don't know where we're going, but we're making great time!" How can you be making great time if you don't even know where you are going and where you are supposed to be going?

The best disappearing act is when we let go of ourselves and the things and people we tend to hold on so tightly to and seek out the bigger picture. We disappear from life being all about us and focus the attention on the One who created us and put us here on this Earth. All of our selfish desires and self-centered attention fades away in this moment, and people see a love that transcends our human nature. For me, my faith in Jesus Christ has sustained me and has served as the foundation of my life here on Earth. I always thought – at least for 3 and a half years of my life – that I would be like my dad. Every boy and some girls aspire to this goal at some point in their life. When my dad made a choice to disappear on his only son and his wife, everything changed. The disappearing act that he chose was not for me, and I made a commitment that I would never make that trick a part of my performance. I chose a different disappearing act. My act was to disappear from myself and allow the love of God to shine through. This act seems harder to me, because I keep wanting to come out from behind the curtain and make life all about me. What I have found is that if I leave that part of me behind the curtain, a greater life can be found for me and for the people around me. And the life I lead is not because of me, but because of Him.

Moments

5

A Mountaintop Moment

This was the first big race of his career. The rest of his team was counting on Kyle to deliver in the biggest event of the day – the 400 meter run. He had never competed at this level and on such a big stage. Many generations had come before him to test their greatness and pursue the crown. He definitely wanted to uphold the legacy of the past and determine his own destiny. How would this day unfold?

The day began like any other day. A breakfast of champions. An encouraging word from his mother. A jab or two from his brothers followed by a courageous challenge. It usually took a long time for his brothers to get in their two cents due to the large nature of his family. He liked having the advice and good-natured ribbing of 4 brothers. The final person to speak with him was his father. "I am proud of you. I love you. I believe in you. Go have the race of your life!"

His father had always been there for him. Every practice. Every game. Every race. And when he needed someone to help him understand the substance of life, his father was there. He didn't see that everywhere. Some of his friends didn't have fathers. Other friends had fathers, but they weren't always there for them. He sat back and contemplated the final words his father had spoken. Four words seemed to reverberate through the chambers of his heart. I BELIEVE IN YOU! Four words that would give him the sustenance to tackle any challenge he would face today.

He pondered the words that were spoken earlier this morning as the other contestants took their place at the starting line. With everyone looking on, he pondered the moment that was before him. What would this moment hold? Would it be a joyous moment? Would it be a mountaintop moment or a valley moment? Would it be a defining moment or a missing moment? Would Kyle make the most of this moment?

Kyle anxiously awaited the start of the race. It was field day at his elementary school. It was time for the 400-yard dash. While not the Olympics, this moment was everything to him. Finally, a chance to follow in the footsteps of his two older brothers. A chance to leave his mark and create a path of his own. He was not built for this race, but he was meant for this moment.

He remembered the words of his parents at the breakfast table a few hours before the race: "We believe in you!" These four words of affirmation provided a solid source of encouragement for the race ahead. It seemed like a monumental task – a lap around the big loop. He was aware of the loop but never in this context. There had been countless days where he had played inside the loop. It was a crushed gravel track that encircled a big field. He had seen older classmates run around this track many times. He had witnessed his older brothers dash around the track with lightning speed. He had even played in the big field in the middle during countless hours of recess and practices for baseball and football.

Somehow, the loop seemed a lot bigger now. The view from the starting line was very different than the view from the middle of the field. In life, our hopes and dreams can seem very distant like a star in the heavens. We set our goals, look at them, and wonder how in the world could we ever see such a thing coming true. Kyle wanted desperately to succeed. Would he come in first? Would he be the last one to finish? Would he finish? All these thoughts raced through his mind violently like a northern wind that whips through the air. He quickly gained his composure and focused on the task at hand. He glanced over at the other competitors. They looked scared and nervous as well. Even his good friend David seemed a bit apprehensive. David was a tremendous athlete with exceptional skills and excellent speed. Kyle and David had played several sports together including football. Kyle usually was the one setting a block for David as he zipped down the field scoring touchdown after touchdown. Kyle knew how fast David was and how he was made for this race. David had both speed and endurance. He wondered why David might be nervous in a moment like this.

Kyle stole a look at the fans who were watching the race. This event was a big deal at field day. Any time you see a gathering of competitors in any sport, people tend to flock to witness the results. His mom was there to cheer him on to victory. She issued her normal vocal words of encouragement. In a resounding voice, she exclaimed, "Way to go Kyle," as if he had already won the race. It as if she was saying, "I believe in you," "You are doing a great job," and "I know you are going to finish strong and achieve your goals," all in one phrase.

Kyle smiled and felt the butterflies float away. His dad had taught him to appreciate moments like this. He often said, "Son, if you have the opportunity to participate in a big moment – and you will, whether in sports or in life – you might as well enjoy the moment!" Enjoy the moment! It was a principle that Kyle's dad emphasized when discussing moments in life. Kyle was now in a moment where anxiousness competes with enjoyment.

Principle 2: Enjoy the Moment

The second principle for maximizing the moments in your life is: Enjoy the moment. Appreciate the opportunity you have been given. Big moments occur at work, at home, on the athletic field, in your community, and around the world. Every

Principle Two:
Enjoy the
Moment

67

day, you are faced with moments. Moments of triumph and success. Moments filled with anxiety and stress. Moments packed with promise and potential. Whether you are running a big race, competing in a championship game, leading a project team or business, encouraging your best friend, or serving your spouse and family, you will have the opportunity to perform in a big moment. Do you enjoy these moments? Or, are you letting fear and stress trap your potential to be the kind of leader others need you to be? Are you letting anxiety steal your opportunity to do the kind of things that only a leader can do?

To enjoy the moment, I have found three key supporting concepts that can make this principle come alive in your life:

1. The journey is as important as the goal
2. Love who you are
3. Love what you do

The Journey and the Goal

First, the journey is as important as the goal. We can become so preoccupied with the destination that we miss the experience of arriving. We become so locked in on the goal that we miss the opportunities along the way. The milestone moments get shoved aside for the "greater goal." We accomplish some things, but we never grow in the process. This limited view inhibits us in two ways. First, the goals that we can accomplish in the future are incremental at best. When we don't consider the journey an important part of the process, we become transactional. We get tasks done, which is important, but we never grow our capacity to be more and do more. In fact, we repeat experience. This repetition can last for years. Repetition is important in practice; it can become extremely limiting in the development of goals.

A business executive was recently reviewing the resume of a prospective employee for a job interview and made the following statement about the repetitious nature of the person's career: "It appears as if he has had 10 years of experience, but the reality is that he has had 1 year of experience repeated 9 times." When you think about your life, would that be said of you? As a father, do you have 10 years of growth, or one year of experience repeated 9 times? As a spouse, do you have 10 years of growth and expansion in developing the most important human relationship you have, or one year of encounters repeated 9 times? As a business leader, are you growing in your career or going through the same motions year after year? As a friend, are you encouraging and challenging the people closest to you, or repeatedly going to the same places and having the same lame conversations? As an athlete, are you challenging yourself to go farther each year, or resting on the laurels of your past trophies collecting dust on a mantel?

Choosing not to respect the journey can also inhibit us from making an impact in the lives of other people. We are so focused on the goal that we miss the purpose of the moment, which always includes the opportunity to touch someone in the process. We are relational beings. We leap out of the womb crying out to connect with someone. Having witnessed five births of my own, I never saw one of our baby boys climb out of the crib and say, "Get out of my way! I've got stuff to do!" They were crying to be comforted, to be held, and to be in relationship with another human being.

According to research reported in the June 2006 issue of the American Sociological Review, Americans are only close to two people. These numbers went down from survey results reported in 1985 where Americans exclaimed they were close to three people. Somewhere along the way, we lost the ability to relate. Or better said, we chose not to relate. Instead of focusing on the process of reaching our goals, we become more narrowly focused on ourselves. This limited view can happen in the context of a single moment or our whole lives. How many moments to impact someone have you missed because of a limited view of life?

The journey is as important as the goal. You must set goals. The best people I coach are the ones who set specific, challenging goals and have a burning desire to accomplish these goals. You are four times more likely to accomplish your goal just by writing it down. The other side of this coin is the journey. You must enjoy the journey!

Consider the following questions when pondering the concept of the journey:

- What did it take for you to reach your goal?
- Who has helped you along the way?
- Who has been impacted by your journey?
- How did your journey affect your growth as a person?

These questions can be phrased in past, present, or future tense to help you recognize the significance of moments and allow you to enjoy the process of accomplishing your hopes and dreams.

Love Who You Are

I wish I had more hair. I wish I was taller. I wish I could sing and play the guitar, keyboards, and drums. Sometimes, I find myself obsessing over these thoughts and more. I would love to be more patient at times. I wish I said the right words to my wife and my boys 100 percent of the time. I stop and wonder why I was created and formed in this fashion. I question characteristics, qualities, and features that even my closest friends would never notice. Maybe, you can relate to the feeling of loving someone else more than yourself. The ideal you that you wish you were!

While these moments are few and far between, they can happen, and they can draw us into a death spiral that can erroneously affect how we feel and what we think about ourselves. If we venture down the path of discontentment, we can find ourselves on a slippery slope that facilitates a free-fall away from the summits in our lives. The right path is important in our thoughts and in our actions.

When I have these thoughts, I realize they are really feelings that are misdirected. It is as if someone is trying to misguide me away from the truth in my life. Feelings can be a perfect tool in this deception. For the women who are reading this book, you know what I am talking about. For the men in the audience, the concept of feelings may seem very foreign to you like a different language. Men, you do have them whether you recognize it or not, and comprehending the concept of feelings can be a great thing, especially when relating to the opposite sex.

Whether we realize it or not, feelings are used against us to deceive us from loving who we really are. Feelings can come from known as well as unknown places. It might be a careless comment about your appearance. "I didn't know white was now in fashion after Labor Day." "With the size of his ears, I know he doesn't have any trouble hearing." Or, it could be a comment about your performance. "Don't mess this project up like you did last time!" "He's not an 'A' player, because he doesn't fit in." Feelings can also come out of nowhere blinding us to the truth. "I never really liked my hair." "I don't feel loved!" "Maybe, God made a mistake when He created me."

While we are reminded constantly to get in touch with our feelings, we must also reconnect with our thoughts. This process does not involve becoming a totally self-absorbed person who stands in front of the mirror every day and proclaims ten times, "I am a beautiful person! I am somebody!" That technique relies on a superficial kind of knowledge and is similar to the experience of eating cotton candy. You feel a temporary rush until the sugar dissolves, and the lump remains in the pit of your stomach.

What I am speaking of is a process that helps you regain perspective about yourself and the world around you. This process focuses on renewing your mind to the truths of life and the truth about you. When I have feelings of doubt about myself, I turn to the One who created me and discover the truths about Him, which help shed light on the truths about me. I realize that my actions begin with my thoughts, and my thoughts can affect my feelings. Adversely or advantageously. When I act on the truth about God and His truth about me, meaningless questions fade away and feelings become favorable. I realize that I was created for a purpose, and I was designed for a reason. I begin to love who I am, knowing that God had a specific intent in mind when He created me. I accept how He is fashioning and forming me into the person I am to become, even if that means never surpassing the six-foot barrier and losing all my hair. We need to love who we are – not because we told ourselves in the mirror today - but because God said He loves us. We need to acknowledge that He is perfect and that He does not make mistakes!

Do you love who you are and who you are becoming? Do you let feelings affect your acceptance of core truths about your life? If you let negative feelings affect your thoughts and ultimately your actions, you will never reach the mountaintops that are prepared just for you.

Consider the following equation:

$$A = T^2 \pm F$$

Let's unpack this equation. Our attitude (A) equals thoughts based on truth (T^2) plus or minus our feelings (F). We must maintain a foundation of truth in our lives, and our thoughts must reflect these truths. You have a choice in whether to believe what is true about your life, but your decision does not determine its truth. As Dr. Barry Landrum, my father-in-law and pastor, says, "The truth is still the truth even if no one believes it. And a lie is still a lie no matter how many people believe it." What truth is God trying to communicate to you about Himself and about your life?

Feelings can help or hinder you based on how you use them. The enemy tries to affect our feelings, because he can do nothing about the truth. Truth is the foundation of the attitude equation. You have a choice to base your thoughts and, ultimately, your attitude on your feelings alone and the circumstances of your life. Or, you can choose an attitude based on the truth. The most successful athletes I work with have a strong foundation of faith in their life and base their life on truth. They persevere through difficult circumstances by focusing on the fact that God created them, He loves them, and He has a plan for their lives. By focusing our thoughts on the right truths, our feelings will be affected in a positive manner, and our attitude will follow.

I have learned to be content with who I am in every moment, because I know whose I am. I am a child of God created in His image and so are you.

Love What You Do

Who wants to hate what they do? Apparently about 80 percent of the population. According to a Harris Interactive poll (the xQ: Execution Quotient Questionnaire) conducted in 2006, only 1 in 5 people was enthusiastic about their team's and organization's goals. Moreover, only 1 in 5 workers said they understand how their tasks fit into their team's and organization's goals, and only half of the people polled were happy and satisfied with the work they had accomplished at the end of the week. This poll surveyed more than 23,00 workers, managers, and executives across all industries and job functions.

Can you imagine doing something that occupies a significant amount of your time and not being fired up about it? Work can consume up to fifty percent of your time in a typical week. For mothers or dads who take care of their kids full-time, the percentage of time for responsibilities is even greater. Shouldn't you be fully engaged in something that you love to do? Some people never realize they have the freedom to ask these essential questions. Questions such as:

- Do I love my work?
- What are my strengths and talents?

- What do those who know me best say my strengths and talents are?
- What am I really passionate about?
- Do my strengths, talents, and passions line up with what I am currently doing?
- Am I fully engaged in my work?
- On Monday morning, do I have a yearning that I MUST be there?
- Do I make a positive impact?

Asking the right questions takes an act of courage that is sometimes foreign to our daily lives. You are never going to be fully content in life unless you love what you do. This concept is broader than a single area of your life like work. Loving what you do has application in your activities in the community, your church, and the lives of your spouse and kids.

I was eating breakfast the other day with my boys at a restaurant and noticed a father who brought his 3-year old daughter and 5-year old son with him for some quality time and a nice meal. At least, I thought that was the scenario. The look on this dad's face spoke volumes. His face was strained, and the tension pulsated through his body. He would rather have been anywhere but there. It was almost as if his wife had pushed him out the door and said, "Take the kids, and don't come back until after lunch." He could not handle the cries for attention that his kids were demanding. It was Saturday morning, yet he was incessantly checking his blackberry device every moment, paranoid that he was going to miss something important. He was missing something; he just never realized it.

Life is fleeting and happens in a moment. Why spend it doing something you don't really like; or worse, being chained to something you hate? I have known people who spent an entire lifetime going through the motions, never realizing something more exciting was waiting for them on the other side of the right question.

Two Keys to Enjoying the Moment

Observation and Reflection are important activities to help you enjoy the moments in your life. The key question is: Do we take the time and create the space for us to observe and reflect before, during, and after the moment?

Observe

Observing the moment involves an understanding almost foreign to our daily lives. Some people go through moments and never notice the window or door that they have passed through to get to the other side of a moment. To truly observe a moment, you must consider the context. You think about all of the moments that led to this moment. For an athlete, she ponders all of the practices, workouts, and mental training that prepared her for this moment. For a father, he considers the growth – the "ten years of growth" – that prepared him to have a "man-to-man" talk with his son. For a leader, she celebrates the experiences that led to this promotion. She thinks about all the people along the way that helped her reach this summit.

In my life, context has helped bring clarity to me and answer the burning question of "Why?". Have you every wondered why you were going through a moment? Most of the time, we consider the question of "Why?" in a negative context. "Why am I going through this moment?" "Why do I have to suffer?" "Why did he get the promotion instead of me?" "Why can't we have any children?" "Why didn't I win the tennis match?" "Why did this happen to me?" We jump into a vicious cycle of asking the same questions over and over, emphasizing different parts of the question along the way. "WHY did this happen to me?" "Why did THIS happen to me?" "Why did this happen TO ME?" It's almost as if we expected our lives to be perfect and free from worry, trials, and stress.

We live in an imperfect world, and life happens. Some great moments, some challenging moments. Context has helped me understand the negative feelings I often associate with the question of "Why?". Context challenges my assumptions about why I arrogantly feel the urge to ask "Why?", and it redirects my energy and thoughts to new questions. These questions have really helped me in moments of trials (and triumphs):

- What is the purpose of this moment?
- What am I supposed to do in this moment?
- Who am I supposed to be in this moment?
- Who else is impacted by this moment?
- How can I grow in this moment?
- How can God be glorified in this moment?

Asking these questions helps me channel my energy to the right focus. While I may not ever answer the question of why I suffered in a given moment, the answers give me purpose and help me respond to the moment at hand in the right way.

You also have to comprehend the content of the moment. When we truly comprehend something, we understand its importance and meaning. Observing the moment involves understanding the totality of the moment. We have to know what's at stake and what it will take for us to perform. We observe all of the variables of the situation and then zero in on what we can control. Content makes us also consider the question of "Why?". Many times, the content of the moment helps us ask the question of "Why?" from a more positive view. When we truly comprehend the totality of the moment, we begin to appreciate the moments in our lives, even when they are too tough to bear at the time.

Rick Reilly wrote an incredible article in the October 9th, 2006, issue of Sports Illustrated on the life of Patrick Henry Hughes and his dad, Patrick John Hughes. In his piece, Reilly highlighted the story of the "only two-person marching-band member in college football." Together, the two of them play trumpet position number 7 in the University of Louisville marching band. You may ask, "Why does it take two people to play one trumpet?" Patrick Henry, who is 18, was born with a rare genetic disorder that left him without eyes, and with arms and legs that won't straighten. His dad, Patrick John who is 45, pushes the wheelchair to put his son to be in the right spot at the right moment on the field. Reilly also noted the following minor details: "Dad also pushes his son to class, sits with him and whispers anything written on the blackboard. After band practice they go home and eat dinner, then Dad goes to work at 11 p.m., gets off at 5 a.m., sleeps a little and gets up at 11 for breakfast, classes, and band."

Consider the following quotes from the article, revealing the struggles Patrick John and Patricia went through when considering the question of "Why?" about their son. "My wife and I were sort of devastated at first," says Patrick John. "I mean we played by all the rules. We worked hard. She didn't have any alcohol during the pregnancy. Why us?" Turmoil, stress, worry, and, maybe, some anger in the moment.

As Patrick Henry grew up, his parents began to consider the context and comprehend the content of the totality of the moment. They witnessed their son achieve greatness. Moments such as achieving a 3.99 GPA in high school and becoming all-state in band and chorus. Other moments that included singing a duet with Pam Tillis at the Grand Ole Opry, playing piano at the Kennedy Center in Washington, D.C., and producing his own CD. All of these moments culminating with the band director at Louisville demanding that he play in the marching band. At the end of the article, Reilly described the end of the journey of "Why?". "We still say, Why us?" says the father. "But now it's Why us – how'd we get so lucky?"

Every moment happens for a reason. Context and content help us gain clarity concerning the reason. These two elements are crucial to observing the moments of our lives. How are you doing at observing the moments in your life?

Reflect

Once you have experienced moments, you must reflect on these moments. It is the only true way to really enjoy them! There have been times in my life where I did not take time to reflect on the moment and missed the joy of the experience. There have been other times where close friends have had to awaken me to what just happened in my life. They highlighted key events and gave their insight into why they thought a certain moment occurred in my life. Through these experiences, I have been truly blessed. Over the years, I feel like I have grown in trying to reflect on the moments in my life and in enjoying the journey; but I still have a long way to go. Growth is admitting you have never arrived.

True reflection begins with quiet moments where you can get away from the current of life and ask yourself the deeper questions. Reflection takes courage and commitment. Courage to go beyond the surface of your persona and travel deep into the depths of your character, and commitment to learn from the experiences of your life and truly become who you were designed to be. The following questions have helped me discover the art of reflection:

- Why did this moment occur?
- What led to this moment?
- What did I learn from the experience of this moment?
- Am I a better person because of this moment?
- What will I do differently as a result of this moment?
- What will I continue doing as a result of this moment?
- Did I impact people in a positive way during this moment?
- Did I say the right words, do the right things, and be the right person in the moment?
- What has become clear to me as a result of this moment?

Remember my concept of the word *moment*. A moment could represent an instant where you had the opportunity to listen and say the right words of encouragement to a friend or family member. You could also think of a moment as the day or week you just experienced. Moments can also be thought of in larger blocks of time like your year, your life, and generations to come. You can break down the concept of moments into any quantity you like, but the questions remain the same. When your watch shows 10:01 p.m. and you think about the day you just experienced, what are your thoughts? Do you wonder if you made the right choices and worked on the right priorities today? Do you know where the time went? Do you truly know how you invested your time, and was it time well spent? Did you have a filter for determining the right priorities? Did good opportunities choke out the best opportunities?

If we don't take time to reflect, we will never know how we are investing our time and if the return on our investment is worth it. We also will never gain clarity about direction for our lives and course corrections that are needed along the way. Finally, a life without reflection inhibits us from truly enjoying the moments in our lives, because we never take time to stop and think about the opportunity of life itself and all that we have been given and what we have been created to do.

Kyle in the Moment

Back to Kyle and his big race. Did Kyle enjoy the moment? Did he win the race? Did he put these concepts into practice? You be the judge.

Kyle, focused on the task at hand and feeling the support of those around him, listened for the word "GO" from the starter and took off like an arrow heading for its target. He was very determined to get a great head start and sprinted past the other contestants. What you have to understand is that 6-year olds do not have much experience in the art of pacing. Veteran runners understand how to pace themselves no matter the distance. At the age of six, you understand one speed and that is go. Go as fast as you can, even if that means your engine runs out before the finish of the race. And that is exactly what happened to Kyle. While his engine did not exactly run out completely, he was walking by the first turn

of the 400-yard dash. He was not alone as others in the race had tried to employ the same strategy of sprint till you drop. While he was not in last place, he had now relinquished possession of first place.

As he walked around the first turn, he was just hoping to finish the race. Now this is where the race became interesting. His oldest brother Drew just happened to be on the other end of the field for recess with the rest of his class. Drew and his friends were witnessing the big race and noticed Kyle walking at the far end of the field. A lot of times, older kids might make fun of a moment like this, foolishly thinking they know a lot more about running a race and about life in general. This was not one of those moments. As Drew and the rest of his friends saw contestants passing Kyle, they began to chant his name. Drew initiated the chant, and his friends loyally followed suit. "KYLE! KYLE! KYLE! KYLE!" The cheer became louder and louder similar to a cheer that gains momentum in a 70,000-person stadium. It usually begins with a single voice and gains the momentum of the masses. While this crowd was not that big, the crescendo of "KYLE!" became audible and loud enough for Kyle to look up and notice what was taking place. He realized they were cheering for him not because he was leading the race, but because they wanted him to do his best. Kyle worked his way from a walk to a trot to a slow jog. By the second straight away, he was running again and making great progress. He could see his brother and the rest of the crowd waiting for him at the last turn before the finish line. The cheers of "KYLE!" became even louder as Kyle and his fans became aware of each other. The cheering section became even more motivated realizing that their encouragement was working, and Kyle grew stronger and faster knowing people wanted to him to succeed.

As Kyle entered the final turn before the last straight away, he smiled at Drew and the rest of his fans. Cheers, fans, and shouts of encouragement were all a part of field day at his school. What happened next was a moment that had never occurred before in the history of field day. Drew and the rest of his friends began to run alongside Kyle to escort him to the finish line. There was a contestant behind Kyle that began to slow down wondering what all the fuss was about Kyle and wishing someone were cheering for him. Kyle finished the race strong, and the cheering section celebrated his efforts by circling around him. This moment was a mountaintop moment for all involved. For Kyle, he was raised to new heights by the encouragement of others. For the cheering section, they learned a valuable lesson about the art of encouragement. They did not set out to be heroes. They just responded in a moment in the best way they could.

We all need people cheering for us – cheering for us to be our best during the moments of our lives. We need people who encourage and challenge us to unleash our full potential and keep us accountable for reaching the mountaintops of life. Two key questions arise from the story of Kyle. First, do you have people who are helping you be the person you were called to be and achieving your purpose in life? Secondly, are you cheering others to do the same?

Enjoy the mountaintop! Enjoy the journey! Enjoy the moment!

Moments

6

A Valley Moment

"What are you doing here Elijah?"
   - 1 Kings 19:9

Elijah had just experienced a mountaintop moment. Literally! He had just participated in a miracle moment on the top of Mount Carmel. He was up against 450 people and involved in a contest of truth. God delivered in a big moment, and truth was revealed. Victory was accomplished, and Elijah topped off this moment with a short marathon run back to the city, beating a king on his horse-driven chariot. With all of this excitement and appreciation, you would have thought Elijah would have been on cloud 9. Within a matter of days, the scene turned to Elijah questioning his existence and wishing he had never been born. And, by the way, he was sleeping and hiding in a cave.

Elijah was a man of faith who trusted God in every moment. Yet, he was human and found himself in a moment that he was apparently stuck. In all of his human strength and intelligence, he could not find a way to escape this moment. His human nature led him to a place where his faith had turned away from all that was true and sure in his life.

How did he go from being on top of the mountain to a feeling of despair and despondency? Why was he here in a "valley moment?" What led him here, and how could he get out of the valley? Closer to home, have you ever been on top of the mountain one day only to find yourself deep in the valley the next? Did you just slide down the mountain? Valleys can be devastating in our lives. What we do and who we become in the valley determines our ability to reach the next summit in our lives.

Valleys Are Inevitable

No matter how hard we try to avoid it, we will eventually experience a valley moment in our lives. I define a "valley moment" as a moment where fear of the present outweighs hope for the future. Valley moments are filled with fear, doubt, despair, depression, and gloom. When you are in a valley moment, you are uncertain about the past, present, and future all in the same moment. Valley moments represent low points in our lives. We cannot see the forest for the trees, and we feel trapped, lost, and hopeless. Consider the following scenarios:

- A mother throws herself into her kids and their lives forsaking herself in the process. A few years and several daughters later, she realizes she is mentally and physically drained due to self-neglect. She rarely makes the time to work out, run, or read like her former self used to do. Spiritually, there is a drought in her life more drastic than the Sahara Desert. She has deprived herself of the things she needed the most in an effort to serve others.

- A college student realizes after 4 years of college that he has no clue about why he chose to take the courses he did and laments the fact that he did not apply himself more. The faded memories of forgettable parties leave feelings of regret.

- A father throws himself into his career, forsaking his family in the process. He wakes up one day realizing he has no relationship with his son as he drives him to college wondering where the moments went and how 18 years seemed to flash before his eyes in an instant.

- The doctor enters the room and pronounces the dreaded "C" word – Cancer! You wonder why you of all people received this curse after living the healthiest life possible.

- A married couple invests in their individual careers and never takes the time to get to know each other on a deep, intimate level. A house, a dog, and two kids later, they wonder how they got to a place of living in a gigantic house, but a hollow home with no foundation to build a future life.

Whether we acknowledge it or not, the fact remains that valleys do exist. Moreover, you will find yourself in a valley at least once in your lifetime. Sometimes, the valley is formed and fashioned as a consequence of the choices we make. Other times, the valley appears out of nowhere, due to the imperfect world in which we live. When you are in a valley, do you sulk in the valley, sink in the valley, or soar out of the valley? The choice is up to you, and it begins with your attitude and your response in the moment.

Peace in the Valley

Do you have peace in the valley, or do you fall to pieces? It eventually comes down to a matter of faith. First, do you have faith? Each one of us puts our faith in something or someone every day. Every time we get on a flight, we put our faith in the plane and the captains who are flying the plane that we will arrive safely. Every time we drive our car on the freeway, we put our faith in our car and the responsibility of other drivers. Believe me, it takes a lot of faith to drive on the major freeways in my city! We put faith in people that they will not hurt us and that we can trust them. We all have and exhibit faith to some degree in our lives. Faith is the key element to get out of the valley.

We find a tremendous amount of faith in the life of Elijah during a valley moment in his life. Listen to his heartbeat as he expresses anguish after he discovers that an angry queen wants him dead:

> *"He came to a broom tree, sat down under it and prayed that he might die. 'I have had enough, Lord,' he said. 'Take my life; I am no better than my ancestors.' Then he lay down under the tree and fell asleep."*
>
> - 1 Kings 19:4-5

Have you ever been at the end of your rope? A place where you just felt like giving up. A moment where you uttered the words, "I've had enough!" You felt as if you had given your all, and it still wasn't good enough or the aftermath was not what you had expected. Elijah found himself at the end of his rope. A valley moment for sure. And, how ironic that it came moments after he had conquered the world. Well, not him exactly, but God through him. He participated in a big moment, and, now, people wanted to kill him. And, not just any person, but an evil queen who had a lot of power and the ear of her husband the king.

Not only did Elijah say that he had had enough, but he also requested that God take his life right there on the spot under the broom tree. Like George Bailey in the classic film *It's a Wonderful Life*, Elijah was probably wishing he had never been born at all. Can you relate to this feeling? Do you have moments of anguish so severe that you wish you had never been born? It is very interesting to me that Elijah had forgotten the moments of courage and conquest and was dazed by fear and frailty. He could not see out of the valley and possessed no hope for the future.

I can relate to the feelings of Elijah. There have been moments where I felt like I had the courage and confidence to conquer the world as well as the fear and uncertainty that everything was going to fall apart. And I have felt both of these extremes all in the very same moment. I have noticed this struggle in others as well. Great athletes. Great performers. Talented executives. Star employees. Awesome parents. No matter how talented you are, you will eventually face this battle; yet there is one quality that stands out that separates the courageous from the cowardly – the ability to persevere. And for the most successful people I know, faith in God was the fuel that gave them the strength to persevere.

Had Elijah lived that bad of a life that he felt he deserved to die? No! He had been very faithful in pursuing his purpose in life and very intentional about his goals and activities. He had a great relationship with God and was very in tune with what God desired to do in and through him. He also had been involved in some pretty cool challenges like praying fire down on a water-drenched bull and accurately predicting the rain forecast – a feat most weather people get wrong on a regular basis. Why did Elijah feel like expressing such harsh feelings when he had experienced some great, mountaintop moments in his life? I wonder sometimes why I express those same feelings in the quiet places of my heart? Do you wonder sometimes why you feel this way as well?

In this valley moment, God took Elijah to a place where He could get through to him. And the beauty of it was that God spoke to Elijah in a still, small voice. Not a shout. Not a "Don't you get it!!" exclamation. A still, small voice that contained the very power and presence of a God he had put his faith in just moments before he entered the valley. God was in the valley, and He very much knew what Elijah needed in this moment.

Strength in the Journey

God told Elijah to eat and drink and then took him on a journey of 200 miles that lasted 40 days and 40 nights. And isn't it ironic that God brought him to a mountain. The very same mountain that God had met with Moses and had given him the laws for the people to live by.

When Elijah arrived at Mount Horeb, God had a cave waiting for him. Elijah "checked in" and spent the night. The next morning, God asked Elijah a very important question: "What are you doing here, Elijah?" Now if that had been you or me in that moment, we probably would have been saying, "I don't know. You *brought* me *here!*" Elijah responded in this manner:

> "*I have been very zealous for the Lord God Almighty. The Israelites have rejected your covenant, broken down your altars, and put your prophets to death with the sword. I am the only one left, and now they are trying to kill me.*"
>
> - 1 Kings 19:10

Elijah resorted to whining. I don't know which would have been a worse response – our sarcasm or Elijah's whining. When you are talking with God on His mountain, I don't think either one of them is a good choice. It's a good thing God has perfect patience, and He exhibited it in this moment with Elijah. He told him to "go out and stand on the mountain in the presence of the Lord, for the Lord is about to pass by" (1 Kings 19:11).

You know the resorts that have the outdoor screens and show a movie for the family every Friday night and then put on a fireworks display? Well, Elijah was getting ready to see an audio/visual display that would put this kind of show to shame.

First, Elijah witnessed a powerful wind that "tore the mountains apart and shattered the rocks," (1 Kings 19:11). But, God did not appear to Elijah in the wind. Next, Elijah saw an earthquake and then a fire. But God was not in either of these mighty powerful happenings (1 Kings 19:11-12). Finally, Elijah heard a still, gentle whisper. 1 Kings 19:13 says, "When Elijah heard it, he pulled his cloak over his face and went out and stood at the mouth of the cave." He knew it was the voice of God and was awed by a whisper that spoke volumes!

As Elijah stood in amazement and a legitimate dose of fear, God again asked him the very same question: "What are you doing here, Elijah?" (1 Kings 19:13). He resorted to the whining again:

> *"I have been very zealous for the Lord God Almighty. The Israelites have rejected your covenant, broken down your altars, and put your prophets to death with the sword. I am the only one left, and now they are trying to kill me."*
>
> - 1 Kings 19:14

Maybe, he thought God did not hear him the first time. Or, maybe, he thought God was not aware of the situation. There are times in my life when I feel like I have to remind an almighty and all-knowing God of the situation. And, I am sure it comes across as whining. I forget that He sees and knows all the moments in my life, even before those moments take place. At some point in our lives, we all find ourselves shouting responses like Elijah's whining to God. Thoughts such as:

- "Don't you see what is happening to me?!"
- "How could you let this happen – to ME?"
- "Why did he have to die so young?"
- "Why can't we have children?"
- "Don't you know I am hurting and don't know where to turn for the answers?"

It is comforting to know that He has a plan for my life and for your life. God is never caught off guard by something that happens in our lives. God has never said, "Oops! Sorry about that! I didn't see that moment coming. Good luck with that." He is there every step of the way – even in valley moments.

After God patiently absorbed Elijah's whining, God gave him specific instructions about the next moments in his life. He gave him an action plan about the work that He still wanted to do in and through Elijah's life.

God also told Elijah to anoint his successor Elisha. God basically gave Elijah a plan for the present and the future. He redirected Elijah's attention away from his fears of the past and the present and channeled his focus on the hope for the present and the future. God challenged him to remember the past moments where confidence was built and leverage that trust in the moment – both this moment and the moments to come.

When I work with amateur and professional athletes on mental toughness, we focus a lot of our attention on the power of trust and performing in the moment. I work with them to trust their abilities and to let those talents come out. We talk about how fear and doubt trap their talent and how belief and trust unleash their talent to help them pursue their maximum potential. I train my athletes to perform in the moment, leveraging the past moments as an ally, not an adversary.

Does your past weigh you down? Is the past a tipping point or a stumbling block for you? Does your past work as an ally or adversary? Even if your past has been filled with some very deep valleys, you can rise out of the depths to reach the mountain God has in store for your life.

Lift Your Eyes

When we are in the depths of a valley, we must look up, not down. The tendency is to look down. You lose your job, you look down. You extend yourself beyond your means and don't get the raise you expected, you look down. After ten weeks of pregnancy, you discover that the heart is no longer beating, and you look down. You receive the news about a loved one who is suddenly dying of cancer without any hope for the future, and you look down.

Valleys represent the lowest point on a terrain and in our lives. We look forward to the peaks and abhor the valleys. At our lowest point, we silently exclaim, "How long is this going to last, and when is it going to stop?!" The pain in our neck from looking down forces us to finally regain our senses and look up because there is nowhere else to turn. Consider the lyrics of this song by Bebo Norman:

"God, my God, I cry out
Your beloved needs You now
God, be near, calm my fear
And take my doubt

Your kindness is what pulls me up
Your love is all that draws me in

I will lift my eyes to the Maker
Of the mountains I can't climb
I will lift my eyes to the Calmer
Of the oceans raging wild
I will lift my eyes to the Healer
Of the hurt I hold inside
I will lift my eyes, lift my eyes to You."

- "I Will Lift My Eyes," song by Bebo Norman

All of us can relate to mountains we can't climb, oceans raging wild, and hurts we hold inside. These are expressions of the valley moments that we experience. Why not turn to the One who created the mountains, calms the oceans, and heals all of our hurts. When we experience a valley moment in our lives, we must look up. We must lift our eyes and allow Him to pull us up out of the valley.

The Wisdom of Yow

Kay had just heard for the third time the dreaded pronouncement of cancer in her life. Her nasty adversary was back with a vengeance, and she was going to have to endure more treatment. It was the middle of busy season in her profession, and she did not have time for this valley moment – once again! Kay Yow, the courageous and successful coach and leader of the North Carolina State women's basketball team, told her players and assistant coaches that she was going to have to miss sixteen games to undergo treatment. She encouraged them to stay focused on their goals for the season. During the season, Coach Yow's team defeated conference and intrastate rival Duke, who was the number one team in the country and undefeated at the time. Kay Yow returned after her leave to lead North Carolina State to the Atlantic Coast Conference (ACC) championship game and to the Sweet Sixteen in the 2007 NCAA Women's Basketball Tournament.

Later that year, Kay Yow received the 2007 ESPN Jimmy V ESPY Award for Perseverance. This award was established in honor of Jim Valvano, a bulldog when it came to overcoming obstacles and persevering through valley moments. Valvano was the legendary coach who led his North Carolina State men's basketball team to an unthinkable win over heavily favored University of Houston in the 1983 NCAA tournament. Valvano also showed tremendous courage in battling cancer, which eventually took his life. He constantly preached a message of never giving up.

During a video segment on ESPN, Kay reflected on the season and her journey through cancer treatment. "I felt like I had zero control over getting cancer, but I have 100 percent control over how I will respond. From the time I was first diagnosed, I realized this: 'Kay, don't wallow in self-pity. It's OK at moments to have some pity, but swish your feet and get out. Just swish and get out!'"

During her speech she gave glory to her Lord and Savior Jesus Christ who gave her the faith, peace, strength, and perseverance to travel through this valley moment. Kay Yow's mantra on valley moments could be summed up in one phrase: "When life kicks you, let it kick you forward."

The Wisdom of a DJ

When I was in college, I learned the art of being a disc jockey. I have always loved music; I just wasn't ever able to play an instrument or sing very well. This lack of musical talent did not keep me from singing my heart and lungs out in the car and in the shower. A true musician would readily predict that I do not have a musical ear, but what I discovered is that I do possess an ear for music. In college, I found a way to explore this talent by playing music.

I earned money by playing music for dances and on the radio. I loved the challenge of listening for unique beats in different songs and stringing them together so the listener would feel a continuous stream of music. After college, I went a different route professionally, but I never lost my love for listening and playing music. Seven years after college, I was able to explore my DJ abilities again doing an evening show for a local contemporary Christian radio station in Austin, Texas. I hosted an evening show from 7-12 pm.

Like all radio stations, we had a certain format and an hourly schedule that defined the direction for the show. The schedule told us when to play station identifications, when to announce the news and weather, and when to play community service announcements. And, of course, we had a commercial-free segment where we played 20 minutes of non-stop music. I liked this segment the best, because it gave me an opportunity to discover the synergy in the music and string together a great segment. It also gave me chance to take the occasional bathroom break, which is very necessary when you are hosting a 5-hour radio show.

One of the worst fears a DJ has is dead air. Nobody wants dead air. Not the listeners. Not the station manager. Not the sponsors. And certainly not the DJ. Dead air is that dreaded moment when you hear nothing on the radio. No music, no commercials, no news, no weather, no nothing. The silence of dead air can be deafening. As a DJ, you meticulously prepare and plan your every move so that dead air will never happen. You constantly check the sound board and the levels for everything from your microphone to the next song that is gong to play. You rehearse in your mind how the next segment will take place. What you will say, what you will do, and how it will sound.

One fateful summer night, I was coming up on our big segment for the hour – the 20 minutes of non-stop music and my favorite moment of the hour. We typically began this segment at 20 after the hour. As the clock displayed 7:19:45, I rehearsed in my mind how this great moment was going to take place. As the clock rolled past 7:19:59, I launched into my most powerful, deep, and booming DJ voice to announce the next segment. The moment went down something like this:

"And now, get *ready* for 20 minutes of NON-STOP MUSIC. RIGHT HERE, on your station for the *best* in contemporary Christian music!"

As I relished in my achievement, I pushed play on the CD player to kick off the next song. The problem was that I forgot to do something I had done a thousand times before. I did not increase the volume level for the song, and our listeners heard a big, fat nothing. So much for the 20 minutes of non-stop music! Would you settle for 19? I froze in the moment wondering why I did not hear any sound coming from the in-studio monitors. I glanced down at the levels and quickly realized my error. I jumped toward the sound board and hurriedly cranked up the volume level, wiped the sweat from my brow, and hoped the audience thought it was just a long, quiet build-up to a crescendo in the song.

Dead air is not good – on the air and in our lives. Nobody wants to have moments where the song of his or her life does not play. Valley moments can represent dead air in your life. The play button is pushed, but the volume level is at zero. And worse, sometimes it is below zero.

No one wants to experience dead air. Not your friends. Not your family members. Not your co-workers. Not your spouse and kids. And certainly not you! Your life represents a song. What song will you sing, and will you let valley moments keep that song from playing and create dead air for you and for those who are waiting to be impacted by you? Take the advice of this DJ and mix a string of great moments together.

You can use the CAR technique to help avoid long periods of dead air.

<u>C</u>hoice

Make the right choices in the moment. Pray for wisdom about the path that will lead you out of the valley. Usually, when we are in a valley, we have taken a wrong path or found ourselves on a detour that we did not expect. We must regain our bearings, lift our eyes, and trust that we will be led on the right path that pulls us up out of the valley.

Regaining your bearings involves taking time to understand the context of your situation, its meaning, and its significance in your life. This process does not necessarily involve answering the "Why?" about the valley. There have been many moments in my life that I did not discover the "Why?" until much later in life. Some moments I may never fully understand why I went through them. The hard thing is that when I was in the valley, "Why?" was the most important question to me at the time. "WHY?" is a question that can burn your heart and sear your mind if you are not careful.

I am not saying we should not have the freedom to ask the question. After all, "Why?" is a legitimate question. It connotes feelings and facts all at the same time. The key point is that we cannot let it bully us into a perpetual spiral downward that dominates our lives. "Why?" has the potential to do this. I have found more powerful questions that help me regain my bearings in the valley:

What? – What do you want me to do?

Where? – Where do you want me to go?
Who? – Who do you want me to meet?
How? – How should I respond?

These questions help us redirect our energy and attention and allow us to discover answers that will help us persevere through the valley.

<u>Attitude</u>

Attitude can help or hinder you in the valley. It can be your stumbling block or stepping stone depending on how you use it. Attitude determines outlook, and outlook can affect destiny. Am I saying you should just grin and bear it when you are suffering through the most challenging times in your life? No. The reality is that none of us can truly grin and bear it in our own strength – no matter how strong we think we are. I am simply saying that you do have a choice, and you should not choose to seethe and sulk in the midst of a valley.

I am an optimist by nature. I have spent my whole life looking for the art of the possible – in the depths of my parents' divorce, in the midst of a miscarriage during my wife's first pregnancy, in the valley of a summer filled with my grandmother's stroke, my grandfather's demise from cancer, and a return home to find two towers brought to the ground by terrorists. The art of the possible involves turning negatives into positives and discovering opportunity in the center of challenges. A great attitude is not a syrupy concept. It is a real and dynamic activator in your life. Great attitudes do not involve being fake and putting on your "happy face" just because you think you need to. Great attitudes involve being authentic and in touch with your soul. I don't think when God set out to create the world, He said, "I think I will create some people who have a horrible attitude, are cranky every day, complain about anything and everything, and never discover the truth about who they are and who they can become." We get to that place on our own.

Attitude is the first step to allow us to perform in the moment. We can never do anything about the trail that led us to this valley, and the path ahead is only forged by what we do today. A bad attitude clouds our vision, and a great attitude clears our vision to see the road ahead. We have a choice about our attitude, no matter what the circumstances are that surround and, sometimes, engulf us. When I am in the midst of a valley and feel like I can't go on, I turn to my faith in God and ask for His strength and His attitude and outlook on life. I ask for power to persevere in the moment, realizing that it is not me but God who is supplying the power. There are moments that will surpass the physical limits of your capabilities. Who will you turn to when these moments happen? What attitude will you choose in the valley moments of your life?

Response

How will you respond when you are in the valley? Will anyone hear your response? Will anyone see what you do? Your response speaks volumes about you and echoes through the mountains around you.

Sometimes, our responses just erupt from a volcano deep within us. We don't know where it comes from, but we just say or do something without thinking about the consequences or repercussions. Your friend cuts you down, and you respond by chopping them down deeper. Your son does the exact opposite of what you asked him to do in open defiance, and you lash out with an anger and venom that most snakes don't possess. Your opponent in tennis conveniently cheats you out of a victory, and you lose your passion for the game.

Our response can be both mental and physical. It can be both in word and deed. We sometimes never take time to reflect on how we should respond in a given moment. We get tricked into thinking we don't have a choice about our response. A valley moment happens, and we give in to the very first reaction, which is often the wrong response.

Principle 3: Respond in the Moment

The third principle to make your life count for what matters most is: Respond in the moment. Life happens. Circumstances beyond our human control will crash into our lives. Responding in the moment is one of the most important principles when you face a difficult time in your life. Once you have considered your choices and

> *Principle Three:*
> *Respond in*
> *the Moment*

determined your attitude, your response focuses your direction. Responding in the moment is taking one step at a time. Responding in the moment is asking the question, "What is the most important thing I can do in this moment?" and doing it. Responding in the moment centers around perspective. We must gain, or sometimes regain, perspective to truly respond in the right way in any given moment, especially the lowest moments in our lives.

The date was June 1, 2005, and the Houston Chronicle published a photo of a tombstone with the following headline:

With 111 games left to go in the season, this Houston newspaper along with many of the Astros' fans had written them off and left them for dead. Their record fell into a valley of 15-30, and hope was nowhere to be found. I received a call around this time to begin meeting with a group of Astros' players to encourage them and help co-lead a Bible study. My first thought was that I had nothing to say to a group of guys who must have been despondent given all the turmoil that was surrounding them. I thought the last thing these guys wanted was someone who they didn't know coming in and telling them that everything was going to be OK. Everything was not OK! The local paper had just printed a giant tombstone signifying their death with three fourths of the season left to play! Who would want to continue a season that seemed to be lingering in the valley?

I agreed that I had nothing to say, but I knew that God had everything to say. I got down on my knees and prayed that God would use this moment as an opportunity to make an impact in the lives of these players. I prayed that everyone involved with the time that we were going to share would be blessed in the process, and I asked God to give us all the proper perspective on how to respond in this moment.

We met for an hour 2-3 times a month. There were about 10 men involved in our time together. The moments we shared were not about any one individual in the room. We focused our time on studying the Bible and discovering what God had in store for each and every one of us. Perspective was the focus. Not wallowing in the mire of a dismal moment. Not playing the victim card. Not shaking a fist at the sky and shouting an angry "WHY?" from deep within our soul. And not just perspective about baseball. Perspective about life. Perspective about what God wanted to teach them in this valley moment that seemed to be eternal, but, in reality, was only a fleeting, temporary instant. We focused on what was important in this moment and what God wanted to do in and through them in the midst of a valley.

During this time, I developed a handout that I gave to the players about perspective. I have since used this with anyone who has ever experienced a trial or triumph.

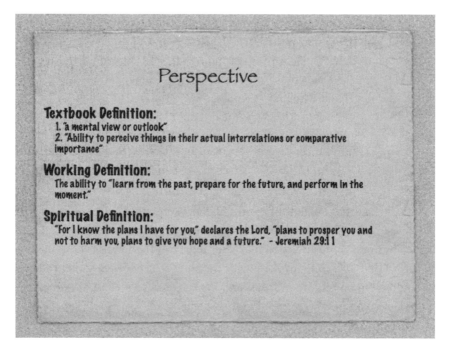

The Astros rebounded from discouragement, despair, and a dismal 15-30 record to finish with a record of 89-73. They won the National League Division and Championship Series and earned a trip to the World Series. What I learned in the process is that responding in the moment takes an active step of faith on our part and a willingness to submit to God's authority and calling on our life. He loves us, has plans for us and has called us to do great things in His name. When you are in the lowest part of the valley, you need to embrace this concept. How do we do this?

First, faith plays a vital role in affecting how we respond in a moment. Do we trust these truths or not? If we do, we will step out in a confidence that transcends human imagination. If we do not, we will take residence in the valley never realizing a better place existed just over the horizon.

Second, friends, family, co-workers, and even strangers can help illuminate the situation and shine the light on what is truly important. Have you ever been in a moment where you were pouring your heart out to someone about the valley you were currently in only to hear a word from them that instantly unveiled the proper response?

Duke University published a study in the June, 2006, issue of the American Sociological Review that cited some startling results regarding our ability to hide from others. The poll stated that "most Americans are close to only 2 people" and that "1 in 4 people have no one to discuss important matters." We must discover and develop relationships with trusted advisors. We can often feed a ludicrous notion that we are self-reliant beings – people who pull themselves up by their bootstraps forsaking any friendship that might reveal the slightest hint of vulnerability in the process. Accomplishments that we think are huge only encourage this kind of behavior. The reality is that we were created to be relational. We need people who will encourage, advise, listen, keep us accountable, and speak truth to us in love. Trusted advisors care about who we are and who we are becoming. A community of co-creators will help you persevere through the valley and achieve your hopes and dreams. Who is on your personal board of advisors? Whose board are you serving on? Who is in your community of co-creators?

Obstacle or Opportunity?

What is the view like when you are in the midst of the valley? Moreover, how do you view valley moments? Kathy Wilburn is a friend of mine who worked as a receptionist for a prominent insurance agency. The title "receptionist" did not do her justice, because she was so much more. She not only answered the phone and greeted everyone who entered the office, but she served as a friend who immediately lifted the spirits of everyone around her. She played a role in the recruiting process of new prospective agents. She also was a master motivator and encourager for the representatives who worked there. It was impossible to pass by her desk without being uplifted. She is very perceptive to the feelings of people. She offers real encouragement – not the kind of fake, syrupy "just feel better" type that usually follows a glue-on smile. Kathy is real, and her advice is based on fact and a keen understanding of what another person needs. Kathy is the kind of person that can help you find your way out of the valley.

Kathy often will give me poems and quotes to encourage me and share with others. I recall one very pertinent quote that speaks to the heart of responding to valley moments in our lives:

> *"Challenges can be stumbling blocks or stepping stones, depending on how you use them."*

How do you use the valley moments in your life? Are they stumbling blocks or stepping stones? Obstacles or opportunities? The valleys in my life have been major opportunities for me to gain perspective and clarity. Clarity about what's important. Clarity about my calling. Clarity about who God is and what He wants to do in and through my life. I have falsely thought in the past that my struggles and challenges were major stumbling blocks for God. What I have realized – sometimes very slowly – is that He views the valleys as major opportunities to show how powerful He is and can be in my life. We do not have to go through valleys for Him to demonstrate His power and love to us; but, sometimes, it is the only way for us to look up and see what He can truly do in the depths of a valley.

Look up, get up, and step up – out of the valley! Respond in the moment!

7

A Courageous Moment

Courage has many faces. Courage is a student making a choice not to drink. Courage is a 15-year old daughter who doesn't give herself away. Courage is a single mother who works to support her children. Courage is a family who adopts a forgotten child. Courage is a leader who does not exploit the system for personal gain. Courage is a soldier who stands up and fights for his country. Courage is a policeman who lays his life on the line every day. Courage is a man who shares his faith when the cost could be his life. Courage is a woman standing up for what is right when others forsake her just because her color is different.

Courage is not talk; it is walk. Courage is not words, it is action. Courage is not just strategy; it is execution. Courage is the demonstration of values, and courage must take place in all areas of your life. For some of us, it may be easier to demonstrate courage at work making the "tough decisions," while we fear having a discussion with our kids about standing up for what is true. We must be courageous in every role in life. Courage should be revealed in every thought, every decision, and every action. Our lives are filled with moments that will test and, hopefully, reveal our courage. How will you respond when the game is on the line?

The Courage Within

Orlando Palmeiro served as the liaison for our bi-monthly Bible studies with the Houston Astros. I consider him a friend and a great example of true courage. I first met Orlando during the Astros' 2005 baseball season that culminated in a trip to the World Series. During that season, we became friends, and I began to see a hidden courage within him.

Before I tell you the rest of his story, it is important to understand a little about the kind of baseball player he is, including his role on the team. Orlando has played for several teams in his career and earned a World Series ring with the Anaheim Angels. Orlando has served as a role player and pinch hitter most of his career. The Astros consider him one of the most valuable players coming off the bench. Around the sixth or seventh inning, Orlando usually gets a signal from the manager to go in and hit for the starting pitcher. Sometimes, it is later in the eighth or ninth inning with the game on the line. The team is basically telling Orlando and the rest of the people watching, we are taking out our stud pitcher and putting our confidence and hope in this player to deliver in a big moment. That is the role of a pinch hitter, and Orlando has met that challenge time and time again.

The man has courage. He defines courage by his actions even in the presence of fear. Fear of striking out. Fear of failing in a moment when everyone is counting on him. Fear that people might question the decision of putting him in to replace the pitcher, especially if he doesn't deliver. He is able to acknowledge the presence of fear and still perform in the moment. While courage in a baseball game is admirable, it can pale in comparison to the courage it takes to journey through life. The fears and trials we face in life can seem like giants when compared to striking out.

An Impossible At-Bat

It was June, 2005, when I first met Orlando. He met us at the door of the exclusive Diamond Club parking lot of Minute Maid Park. We would usually meet there around 2:15 in order to make it up to our meeting room by 2:30. It was a typical June afternoon in Houston – hot and humid.

Orlando had a plastic sack by his side, and he reached inside to hand us a bottled water. I thought surely he had more important things to do than to get us water. What an act of service in a profession where service is usually directed the other way! This was the first of many acts of service that I witnessed amongst Orlando and the rest of the players that we invested in that summer.

As the summer progressed, Orlando shared with me about his father and his battle with cancer. His father spent the better part of that summer in a hospital room in Houston, TX, receiving treatment for a disease that is often not forgiving. At times, Orlando felt helpless. His parents could not speak English, he was on the road half the season and playing games when he was in town, and he received sporadic reports from the doctors. Mentally, it was one of the toughest seasons of his life, and it would last for more than 162 games.

Every two weeks, we would show up at Minute Maid Park, and Orlando was there waiting with his plastic sack of bottled water for us and for his teammates. We would spend time studying the Bible, encouraging each other, and helping the players make sense of a season that began with a 15-30 record. As relationships grew stronger, we began to see a bond that only God could cement. And our focus was much bigger than baseball. We always concluded with a prayer on our knees. Knowing how particular and borderline obsessive baseball players can be, I was amazed at the engagement of the players in these moments. They were focused on this hour and even knelt for ten minutes or so at the end. I doubt many trainers have their players get on their knees for a lengthy period of time before a game.

Every person in the room prayed for the needs of others – both spoken and unspoken. We often prayed for Orlando's father – for his physical and spiritual healing. You see, he had not made a decision like Orlando had, and Orlando worried a lot about this. Orlando had shared many moments with his father growing up, and he credited his dad with being the one who helped him reach the big leagues. Later in life, Orlando had shared with his dad about his decision to be a follower of Jesus Christ; yet his father did not want to make the same decision. At least, not yet. Orlando feared that time would not be on his side.

A Turning Point

We continued to meet with the players as unexplained victories continued to accumulate. The players were amazed at the storyline and a script no human being could have written. While still under a lot of stress, Orlando Palmeiro helped contribute to a championship run that led to a World Series berth. Still, his father remained in worse shape and had moved to another city to receive a bone marrow transplant in the off-season. I was amazed at the focus and determination that Orlando possessed through these moments in his life. He was able to face baseball situations and, more importantly, life situations with a courage not found on this planet. He could have only survived these moments with courage and power from God.

As we began the next season in the Spring of 2006, banners were lifted, rings were passed out, but no resounding triumphs of healing came – physically or spiritually. His dad's condition only worsened. It was a bittersweet time in Orlando's life. In the middle of a deep sea of fear of losing his father, Orlando demonstrated courage. He continued to play hard and pray hard. He prayed for physical and spiritual healing of his father, and he continued to find moments where he could share with his father how Jesus Christ had changed his life. His father still agreed to disagree on this point. It may have been fine for Orlando, but his father felt like he did not need God in his life.

The turning point came in July of 2006. The Astros had just returned home after completing a series with the Texas Rangers. I received a call from Orlando on Monday, July 3rd, and I could sense the angst in his voice. He wanted so badly for his father to know Jesus, and he began thinking that his father's days were numbered. I listened and offered some words of encouragement for him to keep sharing his faith with his father. As I hung up the phone, I became burdened like never before. It was not like I had not been serious about praying for his father's spiritual healing in the past, but the level of intensity rose to an all-time high. I had trouble sleeping that week, and I found myself constantly on my knees – burdened for Orlando, his father, and the rest of his family.

On Friday of that week, we pulled up into the parking lot of Minute Maid Park for our regular time of encouragement and Bible study. But this day was no regular day. As Orlando opened the door to let us in, I noticed the sack with the bottled water. I also noticed there was something different about the expression on his face. His face was almost glowing, and I had never seen this ballplayer's face glow.

As we stepped onto the elevator to go up to the suite level, he turned to me and said, "Well, my father accepted Jesus Christ into his life last night. And he prayed the prayer twice – in English and in Spanish – just to make sure he got the words right and that nothing was lost in translation." We laughed, cried, and high-fived all in the same moment. What a journey! We had a great time that day celebrating a triumph that transcended the ball field below us.

The Rest of the Story

Three weeks later, Orlando Palmeiro's father passed away, finally succumbing to the cancer that had brought both trial and triumph. Orlando took a bereavement leave for a few days and then returned to join his teammates for the final stretch of the season. He returned with a courage that was even stronger than before. He told me when he returned, "If this is what it took for my dad to finally make a decision about a relationship with Jesus Christ – a relationship that will forever secure his status in eternity – then I can accept cancer." Words spoken from the heart of someone who knew our life on this Earth is but a blip on the radar compared to the eternity that his dad was going to spend in Heaven.

There were many phone calls after he returned where Orlando expressed his feelings of missing his father – missing the man who threw with him in the front yard and encouraged him to be the person and player he is today. He was so happy and yet so sad. Happy that his dad's eternal future was secure; sad that he could not spend time with him anymore. Orlando showed great courage during this time. The Astros began an unexplainable winning streak and battled the St Louis Cardinals down the stretch for the division pennant. During this stretch, Orlando had some incredible moments – moments where he delivered when the game was on the line. In the midst of many emotions, he demonstrated courage and focus and played his heart out.

In late August, I remember having a conversation with him about the moments before him. He was on his way to tying a record for the most pinch hits ever by an Astro in a season, but he was still missing his father. We talked about the thought of his father looking down on him with pride – proud of his accomplishments, proud of his persistence, and proud that he took the time to share his life with his father. Orlando lived his life before his father with respect and challenge. He respected and admired his father for who he had been, but he also challenged his dad about who he could become. Prayer was a big part of Orlando's life during these two seasons, and he exhibited courage in his willingness to share his journey of faith with his dad.

The biggest challenge Orlando faced during this time was that he had not had time to decompress from all of the events this season of life had brought him. While he had returned home to be with his family and attend the funeral for a few days in late July, he had to return to rejoin his team. As you can imagine, many things were pulling at him all at once, demanding his immediate focus and attention. Maybe, you can relate to what he was going through. There is never a good time to lose a loved one, especially when you are in the middle of a moment where you must perform. During that August phone call, I shared with Orlando a principle I had used in my own life and with other athletes and executives I had coached. I challenged him to perform in the moment, the fourth principle to making your life count for what matters most. I told him that he was still here in the middle of a pennant race for a reason and that the man who tossed baseballs with him as a kid would probably want him to give this moment everything he had. There would be time to decompress later.

At first glance, this advice and challenge may seem a bit harsh. At its extreme, it sounds like a "grin and bear it, pull yourself up by your bootstraps" Texas challenge, with no respect to what the other person is going through. To some degree it is, but it is not necessarily you pulling up your bootstraps. For Orlando and for many people, this philosophy is rooted and grounded in faith – faith that God will supply the power as we take each step.

Principle 4: Perform in the Moment

Performing in the moment involves execution. In business and in sports, we understand what it means to execute – to take action, to deliver. I love what Larry Bossidy, the former CEO of Honeywell and author of the book *Execution*, says about this topic:

Principle Four:
Perform in
the Moment

"At the end of the day, you bet on people, not on strategies."

You can plan and put together the best strategies, but, when all is said and written, you have to step out and act. When you develop goals for the year, the next step is execution. When you plan a wedding, the next step is saying "I Do," followed by a series of actions that demonstrate your love for your spouse. When you commit to training for a marathon, you put your training into practice when the race is on the line. Working with a lot of athletes, I sometimes see a tendency in them to dwell on past moments. One of my tennis players hits a great shot, and they stop and admire the power and grace of their shot, not focusing on the great return that their opponent just blew by them. Sometimes, they lose several points and obsess over the lost moments instead of performing in the current moment before them. For my baseball players, they sometimes focus on the strikeout they just endured instead of the ball that just went by them in the field. I work with them to perform in the moment, putting the past moments – both good and bad – behind them.

Performing in the moment involves totally focusing on the moment before you and delivering your best. It does not mean that you will win every race, tennis match, or athletic contest, and it certainly does not mean that circumstances will always turn out the way you planned. Performing in the moment means that you are consistently giving your best effort and can walk away from any moment with integrity, content that you gave everything you had mentally, physically, emotionally, socially, and spiritually.

Performing in the moment is a principle for every role that you have in life. It is not just limited to the athletic field or a cubicle or the board room. We must think of this principle in every role that we have been given and in every moment that we receive. I once heard someone define the word *impact* in the following way:

I

M ust

P ersonally

A

C

T

If you read this word as a crossword puzzle, you receive a picture of how to make an impact. To make an impact, you must personally act. No one ever made an impact by lounging in a recliner. If you see a need, do something about it. If you feel someone is hurting, console them. If you are a leader, lead. If you are a spouse, live your vows. If you are a parent, provide encouragement and guidance to your children.

The only moment that we truly have is the current moment. How are you performing in this moment? Especially during major trials in our lives, performing in the moment takes a lot of courage – a quality that we cannot often find within ourselves. Some moments demand a courage that transcends the limits of our human qualities. Where do you look for courage to perform in the moment?

A Mother's Courage

The thought of going back to work scared her to death! How did she get here? Why was she in this moment? Becoming a divorced, single mother was not in the plan. How was she going to live, work, and care for her son? This journey was not one she would have chosen, but the moment was before her, and it would take all the courage she could find. Merriam-Wesbter's dictionary defines *courage* as "mental or moral strength to venture, persevere, and withstand danger, fear, or difficulty." She was in a moment where danger, fear, and difficulty was smacking her in the face, and she would need a supernatural amount of mental and moral strength to persevere in and through this moment. Not only would she need this for herself, but also for her son.

I witnessed firsthand a valiant example of true courage. My mom defined courage by the life that she lived and the humble way that she went about living her life. Truly courageous people do not have to talk about how courageous they are; they demonstrate it through their life. And the truly enlightened ones know and acknowledge where their true courage comes from.

We were at a crossroads in our life. Two people now faced with the challenge of survival, and one depending on the other to ensure that everything was going to be all right. My mom decided to return to teaching – a profession that she was wired to do. Great teachers give of themselves and pour their heart into the heart of another person helping them become all they can be. The truly talented teachers help their students envision possibilities and seize opportunities.

My mom was a master at helping her students discover the art of the possible, and it began with me as her number one pupil. As I grew up, I never knew how close we were to not making it from month to month. She was always positive, even when the threat of not being able to pay the bills was looming in the final days leading up to the next monthly paycheck. We never lacked for anything, and she worked hard on a teacher's salary to provide for me. She sacrificed her needs for mine including clothes, time, gifts, and whatever else a little boy dreams of receiving.

Our existence was a logical one. I never imagined anything different. It was natural, and she worked hard to help me turn a negative situation into a positive one. Not once did I hear her criticize anyone. Not my dad, not God, not other people. I never heard her show resentment for what other people had not only in terms of resources, but also in terms of relationships. She constantly and consistently told me that God had a plan and purpose for my life, and I believed her. And she believed in me.

"I believe in you!" – four words that can make a significant difference in the life of a person, especially a boy growing up in an unusual way. I never lacked for encouragement, and this belief led me to seek a belief and faith that has sustained me for my entire life. Not a belief in myself, but a belief in God who became my Father – earthly and Heavenly. As I came to know Him from the tender age of seven, I understood His love and how He wanted to become my Father.

For some of you, this may seem hard to understand. I mean, it was not like God was shooting jumpers with me in my backyard. He was not telling me to go long and throwing a perfect spiral like Peyton Manning to Marvin Harrison. He was not taking me to the diamond and teaching me to throw a fastball like Nolan Ryan. And yet, He was doing all of this and more.

Growing up as an only child, I spent hours playing outside by myself. On the basketball court, I would imagine playing as all five players on the court, dribbling around and throwing a pass to an area where I would run to, catch the pass, and make the game-winning shot. In our front yard, I would be both quarterback and receiver, throwing my Nerf™ football down the field and running as hard as I could to catch it. And God was with me every step of the way. I felt His presence, and I never lacked for anything.

As I grew up, I had the unique privilege of attending the same high school where my mom taught. Now, some of you might be questioning the word "privilege" and substituting words like "hardship," "hassle," "inconvenience," and "misfortune." High school is an exciting time in your life, and some people may not want their mom being at the same place where rumors run rampant about who you like and why you did not ask a certain girl out and what you made on the science test. You wouldn't want her to hear about these things in the teacher's lounge before you had a chance to explain. The other disadvantage could be that your mom is the teacher nobody likes, and, worse, everyone fears. You know the teacher I am talking about. The one everyone says not to get, and the one you wonder about whether she has any heart at all, much less a life outside of school. Fortunately, my mom was not "That Teacher." She was one of the most popular teachers – the kind everyone wanted. And not because her class was an "easy A." She was liked, appreciated, and respected, because she cared about her students both inside and outside the classroom. The affection students had for her made my transition to high school a blessing.

The word *courage* is derived from the Latin word "cor," which means "heart." Literally, the word courage means to have heart and to give heart to another person. My mom truly exemplified courage and lived out its definition every day of her life. I saw a great example of what it meant to turn negatives into positives, to turn obstacles into opportunities, and to consistently look at the art of the possible instead of the stress of the improbable. She instilled in me a belief that has sustained me for my whole life. She literally gave me heart to continue my life – the courage within to face whatever challenge may come my way. And the coolest thing is that the courage she gave me came from above – a courage I could have never imagined or invented. And the story continues and unfolds in the lives of my boys, and, hopefully, for generations to come.

Where does your courage come from when you need it the most? Who needs you to be courageous in the moments of your life? Will you perform in the moment?

How Do We Perform in the Moment?

Performing in the moment requires commitment, focus, discipline, and action. You can apply this principle in every area and role in your life. When you think about your roles and responsibilities in life, here are some practical thoughts around what it means to perform in the moment:

- **Take responsibility for your actions**
  You are a steward of the moments you have been given. The choice is up to you whether you will be the right person and say and do the right thing in the moment. Being responsible for your actions involves understanding that you have the ability to respond in any moment. The question is, "Will you?"

- **Execute – Execute – Execute**
  I have already mentioned the importance of execution. After you have considered the right strategy, you must execute. The best laid plans remain the best laid plans until we put them into practice. A dream becomes a legacy, if and only if, you are willing to perform in the moment and advance the dream daily with the moments you have before you.

- **Be and do your best in the moment**

  We often think about "doing," but we must give equal consideration to "being." It is been my experience that when I think about and work on the person I am becoming, the "doing" seems to flow out of this. The new math is: BE = DO, where my "to do" list flows out of the person I was created "to be." The sooner I get in touch with and develop my "to be" list, the quicker I can get to the "to do" list, and eventually the "Done" list. Performing in the moment must consist of being and doing your best in every moment.

- **Give 100% effort and focus**

  Some people like to talk about giving 110 percent (or sometimes even greater.) I love how John Wooden, the great UCLA basketball coach, used to correct his basketball players about using this kind of false terminology. He was very specific in his language and taught his players that they could never give more than 100 percent. He further instructed that if they drifted or coasted for all or part of a practice or game they could never regain that time. For example, if they "goofed off" for 20 percent of the time, the maximum effort they could achieve for that particular practice would be 80 percent. You know this concept very well when you think of tests you have taken in school. If there are ten questions on the test, and you choose to only participate in 8 of the questions, your score, at best, can only be an 80. It is important to think about this when we think about our lives. Performing in the moment requires giving 100 percent effort and focus in every moment – not just at work, not just at home – but with our whole life for a lifetime. At the end of your life, what score will you achieve?

- **Be content with the results, knowing you gave your all**

  Some people refer to this point as "integrity in the moment." If you truly perform in the moment and give it everything you have and everything that the moment deserves, you will be content with the results. I reinforce this concept with my athletes constantly, and it helps to take much of the unnecessary pressure that we artificially place on the moments in our lives.

- **If you are in the moment, live in the moment**
Who wants to go through a moment and miss it? The worst thing in our lifetime would be to have the experience and miss the meaning. Now, I realize there are times that we wish we were not in a certain moment, and we wonder how to get out of it. But even in these moments, we must persevere with courage knowing that everything happens for a reason and there is something better on the other side. Performing in the moment involves fully living in the moment and making an impact in the lives of other people.

8

A Powerful Moment

It was September, 1990. A young, 24-year old man was planning and preparing to pop the big question. The couple had discussed the "M" word several times over the past year of dating, but she did not know if and when he might ask her. He had discussed the matter with her mom and dad and had received their blessing. The only thing left was for him to propose to her. You often hear stories about elaborate ideas and ways to ask for a girl's hand in marriage. It could have gone down in this manner.

She calls him up to see what he is doing. He calmly replies, "Watching the game. Why don't you come over." When she arrives at his apartment, he coolly tells her, "Come in, it's open." She enters a room filled with clothes all over the floor and plates and boxes from last night's pizza fest all over the tables and floors. He barely acknowledges her as he remains focused on the game at hand. She pushes an empty pizza box aside and sits down on the couch by him. As his eyes deeply gaze into the high-definition picture before him, he picks up a piece of cold, leftover pizza and casually says as he chews, "You wouldn't want to get married, would you?"

Before the women put down this book in disgust, this is not the way I proposed to my wife. Nor did I at any time consider this approach. I wanted to her say "YES!" I wanted her to experience a great moment! We're talking about ENGAGEMENT! Wouldn't it make sense that you would be fully engaged in the moment? Here is how that September day actually went down.

I planned all of the logistics for several weeks. I reserved the worship center at our church, which took pulling some strings given the amount of activities that took place there. I had written clues on poster board that I put in her room and her house that would lead her on a scavenger hunt through the church and eventually to the exact pew and seat where we first met. I arrived in plenty of time to prepare a song that would play on the huge sound system the moment she sat down.

I was hiding in the sound booth as I heard a door rattling. She was trying to enter through the wrong door. I had left one of the doors unlocked and tried to leave enough clues to guide her to it. As I anticipated the moment, I thought about all of the great and tender moments that had occurred to lead us to this day. She eventually found the right door and sat down at her appointed place. I pushed play on the CD player and Steven Curtis Chapman's "I Will Be Here" echoed throughout the worship center. The words of this song communicated all my heart felt for my future wife. I wanted to be here, there, and everywhere for her. I was communicating to her in the moment: "I will be here for you and for our kids, if we are fortunate enough to have them, in every moment – fully engaged and fully present."

As the song reached its climax, I stood up, walked over to the woman of my dreams, went down on one knee, and popped the question. She said, "YES!" Thank God! Especially when you go to all the trouble to try and plan for a moment such as this. As a side note, some people entered the worship center as the music began playing, and I had to wave them away without my future wife seeing me. But other than that, the moment went according to plan and was more than I could have imagined.

We got married in April, 1991, and have had an incredible journey together. Our moments have been filled with happiness, accomplishments, trials, 5 boys, a miscarriage, some near misses, twists and turns, joy, and a faith that has provided the foundation for us to enjoy the journey. I wish I could say that I have been fully engaged every second of every day of this journey. The truth is that there have been moments when I have been distracted, absent, and given less than my very best. It has not been intentional, but more as a result of being human and dealing with the distractions of life that compete for our time. I have tried to reduce the gap between knowing and doing which is a giant step toward the principle of engaging in the moment, the fifth principle for making the most of the moments in your life.

Principle 5: Engage in the Moment

When a man proposes to a woman and she says yes, they become engaged. He is incredibly focused on the moments leading up to this question and fully present in the moments leading up to the big day before them. This focus transcends his human imagination. There are days when he has to have an opinion about flowers and tall

Principle Five:
Engage in
the Moment

chocolate cakes with layers of strawberries cascading around it when he just wanted to have a cake in the shape of a football. He must learn to walk the delicate balance between caring and not caring too much. Between giving an opinion and deferring to her wishes. This scenario demands being fully present.

After the wedding and ensuing honeymoon, conditions can change causing the two to drift apart. The work really begins, and if you are not careful, the relationship can become transactional in nature. For example, a husband and wife who both work might give the best of themselves at work and serve leftovers to their spouse. For others, they might go through moments, but forget to enjoy, experience, and appreciate the moments as they occur.

Even if you are not married, or in a relationship, or even close to getting engaged, you know people who are. You have heard of the word *engagement* and know the commitment level it requires. When two people get engaged, they become incredibly focused on each other. Some of you know what I am talking about, because of the change you experienced once your best friend popped the question. You used to hang out all the time, but he became so into her that you never saw him anymore. You used to go eat or play basketball together, but, suddenly, there was another checkpoint in the process. In the past, you received a quick "Yes"; now, he says, "Let me check with her," or "No, we have to pick out our china pattern." *China Pattern*? Since when did he become interested in china? Love will do that to a man enticing him to trade hoops for housewares.

The engagement period is a great reminder of how we should approach life. Focused, committed, determined, passionate, caring, and giving every moment our very best. Is that how you think about the moments of your life? Can you relate the focus of an engaged couple to your zeal for life? Are you engaged in the life you are living, or are you just going through the motions? Dictionary.com defines the word *engage* in the following manner:

" 1. to occupy the attention or efforts of a person or persons
2. to attract and hold fast
3. to attract or please
4. to bind, as by pledge, promise, contract, or oath; make liable "

There are several ideas found in this definition of the word *engage* that I think are important to unpack. First, we see the concept of attention and effort. Life requires our attention and effort. The definition says "THE attention and efforts," not just some or a little bit or once in awhile. THE means ALL. The moments in our lives demand us to be engaged. We must experience every moment with eyes wide open. We must focus our attention on the context, content, and components of the moment. Context involves everything that led to this moment. Content involves performing in the moment. Components involve the events and people who are involved in the moment. Our effort should be 100 percent. Not 80, not 110, but 100 percent. You can never give more than 100 percent in a practice, in a game, or in life. It is mathematically impossible to give more than 100 percent effort; but you can choose to give less.

Who would want to give less than their very best effort? I know these people exist, but I try to avoid them at all costs. The truth is that most of us desire to give our very best in every moment, but the dream doesn't always become a reality. We cruise, we coast, we get distracted, and before you know it, moments have passed us by leaving us regretful that our effort was less than 100 percent. This reality can exist in many forms:

- A father goes through life working, playing golf, and occasionally showing up for a family dinner and a piano recital.
- A college student enjoys the freedom of the first two years bypassing a chance to make an impact in his or her world.
- A mother gives all her time to her kids neglecting her spouse and their relationship in the process.
- A pastor preaches great messages on Sunday but experiences a relational deficit with the One he is talking about and the audience he is communicating with the rest of the week.
- A leader ignores his flock of high potential leaders never helping them reach their full potential.
- An employee shows up every day, collects a paycheck, never realizing there was something more waiting to be realized and discovered.

The Discovery of Drew

Drew was a young professional who was on the fast track to success. He was intelligent, both intellectually and emotionally, and had already received the praise of his peers and his promoters as a high potential leader. He was active in his community and his church and always gravitated toward positions of leadership. As a part of his daily routine, he always stopped at his neighborhood Starbucks. As a side note, is there a neighborhood that does not have a Starbucks? They knew him and always greeted him with a friendly "Hello, Drew!" as soon as he entered through the door. They also knew his favorite coffee drink and had it waiting for him. Drew always greeted the baristas and workers by name. Occasionally, he would stay to read the paper, or a book, or spend time journaling and writing. The conversation with the Starbucks employees was surface at best, and he never engaged the people around him in conversation. Why should he? He had his friends in the places he was loved and admired, and he viewed the "coffee crowd" relationships as transactional in nature. He was not selfish in attitude; he just never viewed this interaction as anything more. He ordered a Grande, triple-shot, extra hot latte, exchanged pleasantries along the way, and paid for his drink. A great transaction – nothing more, nothing less.

The reality is that this moment occurred every day like clockwork. He always showed up at 7:07 am. The same barista was always there. Depending on the day, different people were crowded around tables and lounging on the sofa. The high school students on Monday, the tennis crowd on Tuesday, the guy conducting the perfect business deal on his cell phone and letting everyone else know about it on Wednesday, the Mothers' Day Out crew on Thursday, and the study group on Friday. Many people with stories, needs, hopes, dreams, worries, and concerns. He was content to keep these interactions at their proper distance never realizing they were in the story of his life for a reason.

One day, Cody, his long-time barista, was not there in his usual spot. In fact, he had moved on in life. Drew asked about his absence, and the manager mentioned that he had moved away from the city to pursue a career in music. Drew felt bad that he did not get a chance to say goodbye. Moreover, he began feeling a deep sense of regret when he surveyed the substance of all their interactions over the last two years. It was like a long rally of tennis shots with no winners along the way. A serve of "Hello," followed by a return of "Hey," back to "What's up," over the net to "Not much," with a drop shot of "You?", ending with a lob of "Not much. Have a great day!" Back and forth dialogue with all the substance of cotton candy.

Drew was displeased that he had never taken the opportunity to discover more about the person who served him the perfect cup of coffee. 252 interactions over the last year, and nothing to show for it but some empty Starbucks cups. He wondered what kind of an impact he had made on Cody. Did he make an impact?

The question is not: WILL YOU impact someone in your lifetime? The key question is: HOW will you impact them? Sociologists indicate that even the most introverted person will impact or influence 10,000 people in their lifetime. 10K – that's a lot of people! We are constantly impacting people, sometimes in ways we never imagined.

Many times, we think a decision not to speak or not to smile has no implications on other people. The truth is that these decisions can have a profound impact on the people who come into our lives. A smile or encouraging word can truly have an eternal impact. I love what J. R. Miller says in the book *The Building of Character*:

> *"There have been meetings of only a moment which have left impressions for life, for eternity. No one can understand that mysterious thing we call influence... yet everyone of us continually exerts influence, either to heal, to bless, to leave marks of beauty; or to wound, to hurt, to poison, to stain our lives."*

10K! Who is in your 10K? How are you influencing and impacting them? You never know who is watching you and the impact and influence you have on them. Use this privilege wisely!

In a typical office building, many people pass each other likes ships in the nights never saying hello. We get in the elevator together and nervously glance at our shoes, our watches, or the floors as the seconds tick off on the display. In some elevators, they have even built monitors to give the headlines for the day to relieve the stress of having to speak to the people next to us. Many people fight to get into the side of the elevator that has the monitor just so they have an excuse not to speak, because they are watching the news which they just read about, watched on the morning news, and listened to on the radio in their cars. We often treat people like we were only going to see them for thirty minutes instead of know them for thirty years. What would our interactions with people look like if we considered each meeting a divine and meaningful appointment of timeless proportions?

Drew's Resolve

Drew made a decision after he heard the news of Cody's departure that he would never again remain on the surface in his relationships with people. Again, Drew was a "Type A" personality with a lot of drive, determination, and focus balanced with compassion and concern to make a difference. Being less than fully engaged was not a goal; it just became a reality over time. He made a commitment to himself to go deeper in all of his interactions. He even evaluated where he thought he was with the most important relationships in his life – his friends, his family, his girlfriend, and his co-workers – and decided that these relationships deserved an overhaul.

He made the choice to engage in the moment. Whatever that moment was – a conversation over coffee, a friendly hello to the guard downstairs in his office building, a phone call to a customer, a holiday card to his parents, a plane ride to the West Coast – he was going to be fully present, bringing all of himself to every moment. By going through some self-reflection, he became honest with himself about the times he had let himself and others down.

We are responsible for the lives we lead. How you are being responsible for the life you lead?

The Lost Art of Attraction

To engage also means "to attract and hold fast." Just like magnets that attract each other, we become attracted to things and people. The key is making sure we become attracted to the right things and the right people and that we hold fast in our attraction. In many ways, we've become a distracted generation whose affections are easily hi-jacked.

- A spouse suddenly becomes bored in his or her marriage and becomes distracted with a new affection.
- A teenage girl has a momentary lapse in judgment, forgets her priorities, and gives herself away.
- An athlete is attracted by individual accolades and forgets his responsibility to the team.
- A leader becomes so attracted to personal financial gain that he forgets to hold fast to the integrity that once governed his life.

We often navigate our lives like Jr. High dating, moving from one relationship to the next – relationships with people and relationships with things. We forsake our first love in favor of the wrong things and the wrong people that are paraded in front of us every day. It is like an all-you-can-eat buffet that constantly invites us to pick and choose whatever we want, because we have the free will to do so. Or the dessert tray at a great Italian restaurant. We made a decision not to partake, but we ask the waiter to bring it out just to look. And, once we see the enticing delights before us, we succumb to the urge to go for it.

Whether it is our values or our priorities or our spouse or our children, we must hold fast to the attraction of our first love. We cannot let the distractions of this world entice us into making the wrong decisions about how we use our time, our talents, and our resources. For some of you, this means a resolve to be more engaged in conversations – with your friends and co-workers, with your spouse or significant other, and with your kids. Early in my marriage, my wife helped me learn that listening to her tell me about her day while watching the basketball game on TV and reading the newspaper was not a talent. Although I could recite everything she said word for word, I was not being an effective and empathic listener, and it took just a few times for her to shut down the conversation for me to learn this concept.

It takes effort and engagement to listen. The average person listens at a pace of 400-600 words per minute. The average person speaks at a pace of 180-200 words per minute. No wonder we become distracted. We have the capacity to listen 2-3 times faster than a person can talk. The amount of gadgets that vie for our attention many times compounds the problem. I hate being in someone's office or at lunch, and the other person responds to the nearest beep, buzz, or blast beckoning for instant attention. Turn off the distractions, and turn on your attentiveness! Engage in the moments that you have with your spouse, your kids, and the people who mean the most in your life. This time is so precious, and we must give it the proper respect it deserves.

For some of you, the concept of engagement means making a commitment to focus on the person or task at hand. I once heard a story of an executive who conducted a recruiting interview by asking questions of the recruit while simultaneously holding an instant message conversation online about tickets for the basketball game that night. We think we are efficient, because we can multitask, but this so-called talent is really just the art of not paying attention. When we choose not to engage, we don't give moments our best.

Sometimes, we are there but not really there. Decide to be there, fully engaged, soaking up all that the moment has to offer. Make memories, not regrets.

Great moments build momentum. How do we make a difference? Moment by moment. How do we add value? Moment by moment. How do we discover and live out our purpose? Moment by moment. How do we make our lives count for what matters most? Moment by moment.

Here are some practical steps to engaging in the moment:

- **Look** – Look at the people involved in the moment. Look at the situation. Evaluate if you are fully involved and engaged in the moment. Are you devoting yourself – all of yourself – to this moment? Remember, you will never be able to regain this moment. The only moment that we have is the current one. Do you see it?
- **Listen** – Listen to everything in the moment. The meaning of words is often found in the unspoken. Listen for what is not being said. Listen for what is communicated beyond the words that are used through non-verbal cues such as tone of voice and facial expressions. Ninety-three percent of the message is communicated

through non-verbal cues. Listen for the melodies beyond the notes that are actually played.

- **Live** – Live in the moment – the essence of true engagement. Bring everything you have and all of who you are to the moment. Don't let any moment pass you by. Bring your best!
- **Love** – Decide to fully engage your gifts and talents in every moment with the intention of making an impact in the life of another person. There is a reason you were created the way you were and a purpose for every moment. Love who you are, where you are, and who you are with.

9

A Purposeful Moment

"Any life, no matter how long and complex it may be, is made up of a single moment - the moment in which a man finds out, once and for all, who he is."
  - Jorge Luis Borges

What's the purpose of my life? What's the point? Why am I here? Am I adding value? Do I make a difference? Relevant questions that everyone asks of themselves at some point in their lives – sometimes on a daily basis. These questions, while important, do not occupy the time and respect that they deserve in our busy, overcrowded, sometimes transactional lives. When these questions arise, we often push them down below the surface similar to the act of pushing a beach ball under water. At some point though, just like the beach ball, the questions resurface stronger than before, springing out of the depths of our lives. They demand an answer!

The funny thing about these questions is that we are very intentional in some areas of our lives about discovering the answers. Think about your job. When you first start a job or accept a new role, you diligently discover what the company is all about and the purpose behind your role. You ensure that you are adding value, and you seek to work on the right things. You strive to make a difference in the lives of your people and your customers.

What about training for something like a marathon? You set a goal and identify why anyone, including yourself, would want to conquer the challenge of running 26.2 miles. You find a training program and mentors who will run alongside you and help you accomplish your goal. You constantly evaluate your times in training and practice races, always keeping the bigger goal in mind. Marathon training programs typically last for at least 6 months. Purpose and passion have to be clearly identified and embraced to endure the rigors of this kind of adventure.

Yet, we can become incredibly forgetful when we think about the bigger picture of our lives. We don't take time to think about the most important questions of our lives. We get caught in little purposes full of activities and transactions instead of an overriding purpose driving towards a life full of meaning and impact. We succumb to a full life instead of seeking a fulfilling life.

What makes us so intentional in these areas and less purposeful in others? Perhaps, success in a race or at work is easier to measure. You win, or you lose the race. You accomplish the time you wanted, or you put in more training until you do. You complete the projects at work. You hit the quarterly sales targets – or not. The time frame for discovering the results is a lot shorter as well. The clock above the finish line does not lie. The numbers tell the story of your results.

In other areas of our lives, success is harder to measure, and results do not often reveal themselves until much later down the road. Everything cannot be reduced to a metric, and impact often takes time. As a business executive recently said to me, "I know how to motivate my sales force, but I am not sure how to motivate my family." The worst thing would be to throw our hands up in frustration and give up.

Being purposeful with our lives takes time and investment on our part. The work may seem hard, but the return is worth the effort. The key question is: Do we want to take the time to discover our purpose? And, are we afraid to even ask the question? My goal in writing this book is to challenge you to make your life count for what matters most and to maximize the moments in your life. This process begins with identifying why you are here.

Why

The first time that I can remember asking this question in a constructive and relevant way was when I was 7 years old. I know I uttered this question before this time. It was probably when I was 2. The two favorite words of a typical two-year old are "Why?" and "No!" What I am talking about is asking the question of "Why?" in a meaningful way – a manner to discover truth, not to defend my own agenda and actions.

My mom and I were watching a program on television, and a man was speaking with great eloquence and grace. He looked at the people in a huge stadium as he spoke words from his heart. While I was not there in the stadium, I knew that he was speaking to me. He said that we were all created for a *purpose* – the first time I had really heard that word. He also said, "God created you for a reason." My mom had told me about God, and I saw God work in her life. I witnessed her faith in something beyond herself, and the manner in which she lived demonstrated that faith on a daily basis. It was great to know that there was someone in control of this broad universe. I was old enough to know that the world I lived in was not perfect and people I was supposed to look up to were not always dependable. I think we all long for others to be dependable – at least one person that we can count on when all else fails. After 7 years of life, my mom and the man on the TV – Billy Graham – were saying that God was dependable, and more than that, he created me and designed me for a purpose.

In that exact moment, I initiated a quest to discover the reason. This process began with accepting the truths about who God was and what He said was true about my life. On that night, I made a decision that totally transformed the rest of my life. I made a decision to accept Jesus Christ into my life, so that I could have a relationship with the one true God who could help me answer the question of "Why?"

Principle 6: Pray in the Moment

The sixth principle to maximize the moments in your life is to pray in the moment. This principle is the most important one and is foundational to all the other principles I have outlined in this book. I love the song "Resurrection" by Nicol Sponberg which echoes a prayer of total transformation:

> *Principle Six:*
> *Pray in the*
> *Moment*

> *I'm at a loss for words, there's nothing to say*
> *I sit in silence wondering what led me to this place*
> *How did my heart become so lifeless and cold*
> *Where did the passion go?*
>
> *When all my efforts seem like chasing wind*
> *I've used up all my strength and there's nothing left to give*
> *I've lost the feeling and I'm down to the core*
> *Can't fake it anymore*

At some point in our lives, we reach a point where we are at a loss for words. We wonder how we got here. We feel lifeless and cold. We miss the passion. We chase and pursue but never reach and grasp. We wear a mask until we can't fake it anymore. The reality is that we often reach this point before we realize it. It's like the alarm clock that beeps loudly for several minutes before we finally realize something is screaming for our attention, and we turn it off.

These moments of awakening happen in the best of times and also the worst of times. A person becomes a millionaire for the first time and realizes that money cannot cure the yearning deep within the soul. A crisis beckons for our attention, and we realize we need something beyond ourselves to help us deal with the pain.

We finally become so clued in that we speak out. We talk to the wall, the ceiling, other people, and anybody or anything that will listen to our cry. We begin to ask questions that we never considered before. Or better said, questions that we pushed down below the surface. We feel a presence within the world and within other people that we are drawn to, and we begin to ask what is different about their lives. Responses include a variety of common solutions:

- "A new diet."
- "A new relationship."
- "A new promotion."
- "The latest, bestselling book."
- "Plastic surgery."
- "Being a good person."
- "Religion."
- "The morning boot camp and spin class."

As you study their responses, you begin to think there must be something else. There are many ways to find temporary bliss, but only one way to find true contentment and joy. And then you find someone who tells you that none of these so-called solutions will bring you eternal satisfaction. Not a new diet, or a new relationship, or a new promotion, or the latest bestseller, or plastic surgery. Even being a good person mixed with religion cannot bring the satisfaction you need. This friend begins to tell you about a God who loves you so much, He created and designed you for a specific *purpose*. Your friend consoles you with the fact that no matter what you have been through or where you have sought contentment in your life, God has plans for your life. The choice is up to you whether you want to accept His invitation.

> *"Here I am at the end I'm in need of resurrection*
> *Only you can take this empty shell and raise it from the dead*
> *What I've lost to the world what seems far beyond redemption*
> *You can take the pieces in your hand and make me whole again."*
>   - "Resurrection," song by Nicol Sponberg

Emptiness can be found in many ways. You fail to get the promotion that was promised. You seek contentment in a relationship only to discover that she was not all that into you in the first place. You work hard on a project that fails. You pour yourself into a bottomless bottle that never provides the drink you really need. You find your fifteen minutes of fame only to discover the spotlight was not that good to begin with. You make the money and buy all the stuff only to realize that excess is overrated.

You realize that you are in need of a complete resurrection – a rewiring of sorts. You search for meaning, direction, and wisdom beyond your human boundaries. Abraham Lincoln said it this way:

> *"I have been driven many times upon my knees by the overwhelming conviction that I had nowhere else to go. My own wisdom and that of all about me seemed insufficient for that day." (Lincoln Observed: The Civil War Dispatches of Noah Brooks edited by Michael Burlingame, Johns Hopkins University Press, Baltimore, 1998, p. 210.)*

President Lincoln recognized a need to pray in the moment. He was surrounded by irrationality and prejudice during an era of slavery and the Civil War. Lincoln was called upon to navigate one of the most crucial moments in the history of our country. Why not seek wisdom and counsel from the one true source?

Prayer has been a foundational element of my life, especially since I first uttered a prayer of confession and acceptance at the tender age of 7. I am sure that my Mom and I prayed when I was younger, but prayer took on a new meaning in this moment. I began to see God for who He really was. When you enter into a relationship with someone, everything changes. Before, it was just someone you passed in the hallway at school or bumped into at Starbucks. After you make a commitment to that person, you begin to notice and appreciate qualities about the other person that you never noticed before. The relationship enters a dynamic dimension that you never could have imagined.

This state is how I feel about my relationship with God. Before, it was someone I just passed by at Starbucks. He was always there, I just never took time to feel His presence. After I made my commitment to Him, everything changed about my relationship with Him, including the sudden realization of His presence with me everywhere I went. It is kind of like the feeling when you buy a new car, and you suddenly see that car everywhere. The first car I bought when I moved to Houston was a Saab 900 Turbo. I never noticed Saabs in the south before. Trucks in Texas are much more prevalent. After I bought the car, it seemed like Saabs were surrounding me everywhere I went.

The Air I Breathe

Prayer is a vital part of maintaining my relationship with God. It is like the air I breathe. Prayer keeps me grounded and centered. Prayer keeps me focused and on track. Prayer helps me stay focused on my purpose and calling in life. Prayer attacks stress in my life and provides a peace beyond my human understanding. Prayer guides me in my decisions. Prayer prepares me for my relationships. Prayer serves as the foundation of my life no matter what the circumstance.

I wish I could tell you that I have prayed every moment since my decision to follow Jesus. I have not. In fact, if I was really honest, there are moments where I have gone in a totally different direction. In these moments, I have relied on MY strength, MY wisdom, and MY desires. I have pursued goals that were not in line with my purpose. I have made choices that were against God's will for my life, and I have suffered consequences for these decisions. I have received honors for accomplishments, and I have made it all about me. I have been asked the question, "What's different about your life?", and I have failed to mention how God factored into the equation.

I am not proud of these moments, nor do I condemn you if you have done the same thing. I have tried to learn from these moments, and make my life more about Him as I grow and mature in my faith. I have sought out and surrounded myself with people who are trying to do the same. We become like those we associate with. If we surround ourselves with people who think life is all about them, we will tend to believe and follow the same principle. If we choose to be sharpened by people who exemplify servant leadership and follow the example Jesus Christ gave us, we will realize that life is not all about us. And this discovery will lead us to our knees.

The moment we realize who God is and who we are is a sacred and special moment. It is the true secret of this life. The worst thing would be to reach the end of your life and realize that you spent your time on the wrong things. If you are a student, you would not want to read chapters 2 and 3 in your Social Studies book only to find out the test the next day is on chapters 4 and 5. If you work for an organization, you would hate to find out that you spent six weeks of your life working on a project only to find out that your boss never thought that project was of any importance. You don't want to spend your life working on the wrong assignment!

How do you discover the right assignment in your life? For me, it began with getting in touch with who God is and entering into a relationship with Him. Once I made this decision, I began a journey to complete the following statements:

- I have been created and placed here on this Earth to….
- My purpose in life is….
- I have been called to….
- I am making a difference by….
- The point of my life is….

I don't intend to make this process more formal or more complicated than it should be. We tend to look at questions like these and throw up our hands in frustration because of their depth and the time it takes to gain clarity about the answers. I have provided these questions for you as a resource to help you become more purposeful and intentional in your life. My desire is that you would seek a place of solitude sometime in the next two weeks and begin to answer these questions for your life. I know that God wants to do amazing things in and through your life. I also know that you and I have a choice in how we live our lives. We can decide to answer His calling for our lives and embrace the reason we have been created, or we can reject His invitation and live our lives however we please. My hope, and more importantly, God's desire, is that you would accept His invitation and invest your time on this earth for what matters most – namely, loving God above all things, worshipping Him with your thoughts, feelings, and actions, and demonstrating this love to other people.

The truly successful and significant people have figured out how to do this in the context of whatever role they have.

CANCER

Ernie was following along in his father's footsteps, proceeding with the same career that had brought his father admiration and recognition. He had achieved a level of success, and the world had recognized him for his excellence. A phone call put all of the recognition into perspective.

"Non-Hodgkin's Lymphoma!" said the voice on the other line. The news was worse than he had expected.

Earlier that day, Ernie had entered the doors of Emory University Hospital to have a tumor checked out. The nurse said, "Let's get you in and out of here so you can go celebrate your anniversary." It was his wedding anniversary, his oldest son was home from college, and Ernie had planned to spend a low-key night watching a movie with his wife and kids. The nurse proceeded to stick a needle in the side of his face. Instead of getting him on to celebrate, the doctor returned promptly into the room and revealed, "Well, this isn't what we think it is! This looks a lot like lymphosites. We'll have to do some more testing, but that's what it looks like to me." Translation: CANCER!

Ernie pretty much knew the hand he had been dealt walking out of the office. Can you imagine his ride home? For some of you, you can. You either have cancer, are a cancer survivor, supported a loved one who is battling cancer, or have prayed for a friend who has had this disease invade the depths of their bodies. A family at home waiting to greet him. A son home from college excited about telling his dad about his experiences over the last semester. All of these thoughts passed through Ernie's mind as he made the trip home. What did all of this mean? What would the future hold?

When he pulled up into the driveway and entered his home, he did not immediately tell his family. After all, the doctor said they needed to do more testing. There was an outside chance that further tests would dispute the initial predictions. But he knew.

The next night, the phone rang after the family dinner. No one wants to receive a call like this. The doctor confirmed the initial prediction of cancer. After Ernie completed a somewhat lengthy call with the doctor, his son Eric came into the room. Unaware of the moments that had just transpired and the dreadful details that had just been discussed, Eric asked, "Dad, we're going down to Blockbuster to rent a movie. What movie should I get?"

"I don't know son. Why don't you get something funny," Ernie responded. Sometimes, laughter is the best medicine for a moment such as this. His wife Cheryl asked if that was Emory University that had called. Ernie answered, "Yeah, and it's not what we thought." The two of them began to discuss what the future would hold.

At a moment like this, reality comes crashing through the door of your well-planned life. And not just reality, but also uncertainty. Questions begin to surface like "What does this mean?", "What's next?", and "How bad is it?" You can't really describe what it feels like. You know you just want it to stop. In a moment like this, everything that you were so sure of becomes like sinking sand. The certainty of tomorrow, the air of invincibility, and the arrogance of immortality all vanish in an instant, and you are left in a puff of smoke with your head spinning from the words that echoed through the phone in a moment.

Within a week, Ernie was going through all kinds of scans, being poked and prodded, drinking liquids that he never envisioned, and giving up bone marrow from his back. Not the type of activities he had scheduled into his well-arranged, neatly-planned life. Ernie endured test after test to see how early it was and if the cancer had invaded his body anywhere else. The waiting was the hardest part. We live in a world of instant results and round-the-clock news. Nobody likes to wait, especially when your life is at stake. Can you imagine discovering you have cancer, not knowing how bad it is, and then having to go through a battery of tests and the doctor saying, "We'll call you in a few days with the results,"? A moment of uncertainty can slowly crush a person who does not have a solid foundation.

"Understanding destination is understanding destiny." A lead-in quote by Ernie Johnson, the great NBA broadcaster and studio host for TNT, that was voiced in the context of an NBA playoff game. But this prophetic quote was much more than a setup line for a game. It was his axiom for life. You see, to really comprehend this moment on August 21, 2003, when he first discovered that he had follicular Non-Hodgkin's Lymphoma, you have to understand the context for the moments leading up to this seemingly hopeless situation.

The Best Decision He Ever Made

"Where do you go to church?" The question echoed across the room from a client to Cheryl Johnson, who at the time was a creative curtain maker. What began as a hobby had now turned into a job, and she was looking into the face of a person she might have never met except for this chance "client opportunity." It was more than chance that brought these two together. Cheryl responded that they currently did not go to church for a variety of reasons. "We have a special needs child, and it is too hard to get him to church and obtain the care he needs."

"That's very interesting," the client exclaimed. "You need to come to Crossroads. I am in charge of the children's area, and I will make sure that your child is taken care of."

Cheryl went home and told Ernie about this bizarre encounter. It was just what they had been seeking, not necessarily for themselves, but for their kids. Their oldest son was thirteen, and they wanted to find a place where their children could grow spiritually. Ernie never expected what would happen on that fateful day he stepped into the sanctuary at Crossroads Community Church. The pastor, Kevin Myers, was preaching a message entitled "Wholeness or Happiness?" It was a question that cut to the heart of who Ernie Johnson had become. In this moment, Ernie felt like he was the only one in the audience and that Kevin was speaking directly to him. "It was as if someone had given Kevin all my files, and he knew the history of my life up to this point," Ernie reflected. We attended for several months, and every message Kevin preached seemed to convict me left and right." Kevin was the same age as Ernie and, like Ernie, he was the father of several children. While Kevin could relate and communicate in a way tailored to Ernie's situation in life, he was really just serving as a conduit for what God wanted to communicate to Ernie about his life.

Three months later after that first fateful visit, Ernie sat down with Kevin at O'Charley's restaurant to reveal the uneasiness he felt in his heart as a result of Kevin's messages. "I think God is messing with me!" Ernie confessed. "I'm seeing a lot of things in my life that I didn't know were there before. I'm seeing a different purpose for my life and that life is not all about me and really all about God." As they talked more about where Ernie's life was headed, Ernie prayed at the lunch table at O'Charley's restaurant in Lawrenceville, Georgia, to receive Jesus Christ into his life. It was THE purposeful moment in his life – a truly life-changing moment.

It was a defining moment in Ernie's journey and prepared him for the moments that were yet to happen in his life. Mountaintop moments and valley moments. Ernie points to this moment on December 10, 1997, and his decision in the moment as a turning point in his life.

Up to this moment in 1997, Ernie described his life as a "ME-Centered" life. The people around Ernie would not have described him as selfish or self-centered. Like so many people, Ernie was just pursuing success never wondering whether his life had a higher calling of significance. He segmented his life and sought to do his best for each of his roles in life in his own strength. At some point, we all reach the limit of our human greatness. At some point, we can no longer lean on our human understanding to explain the reasons we exist. At some point, we have to realize that we are living one life with a variety of roles – not many lives with many competing and conflicting interests and demands.

Ernie had reached this point in his life. "There just comes a realization, despite what outwardly you seem to have in a great job and a great family, that I was missing out on a whole lot more. I was just looking at what made me happy, and what satisfied me. It was always just ME, ME, ME, and it opened my eyes to what God had for me," Ernie revealed. He came to realize that life was more than just how much he could acquire in accolades and awards. He no longer wanted to live a transactional life.

For a major part of his life, Ernie had mistakenly thought of his life in terms of segments – the work part, the family piece, the spiritual segment if applicable. For a lot of people, they buy into this outlook on life as well. Compartments without congruence. Kevin Myers enlightened Ernie's thinking on this and let him know that God never intended for us to live a compartmentalized life, with segments competing for your passions, attention, and time. Kevin described the spiritual part as "the crust of the whole [life] pie" – the foundation of everything you are and do. A true eye-opener for Ernie Johnson. Ernie realized that he was spiritual and that his relationship with Jesus Christ was the cornerstone of everything he did in life. Ernie said, "It meant that every decision I made personally and professionally was a God-centered thing."

He had made a decision, which helped him understand his destination. And by understanding his destination, he now understood his destiny.

Trust God…. Period.

With his newfound faith in Jesus Christ, Ernie began to live a life of significance. God redirected his priorities in a way that helped him find contentment in any situation. Ernie still pursued excellence at work winning 3 Emmys for his work at TNT. The difference was that he was now living a whole life. Excellence at work did not come at the expense of other areas like his faith and his family. He also realized that the glory was not his to steal. Any awards, any accolades, and any success, personally or professionally, was a result of God's blessings and the glory was all His. A huge shift in priorities for a man of many talents!

When friends and colleagues first heard of Ernie's newfound discovery of faith, they did not understand the magnitude of the transformation that was about to take place in his life. He said the standard response when they would come up to him was, "I'm glad you found some peace and that you found God. Now, you can compartmentalize that over here, and go to it on Sundays or Tuesdays or when you're not feeling good." In these moments, Ernie would quickly straighten them out and proclaim, "No, that's not it. This is my whole foundation. There's not a part of my life that doesn't have God in it."

Ernie's mantra became "TRUST GOD…. PERIOD." He thought about it everywhere He went. At the bottom of every e-mail Ernie sends, this mantra rings forth. His work e-mail, a place where the halls of faith never reach, always ends with the phrase in bold: **Trust God…. Period.** He began to put this philosophy into practice everywhere he went, but it wasn't easy. There were battles to be won.

The first test came when Ernie entered a Christian bookstore shortly after his decision to follow Jesus. You would think at first glance that the best place – the most comfortable place – for a new Christian would be a Christian bookstore. But, Ernie entered the store with a horribly uneasy feeling. Ernie felt as if he should put on a phony nose and glasses, because someone might recognize him as the guy on TV and wonder, "What's he doing in here?" He described this feeling similar to the feeling of a man going into Victoria Secret's for the first time to buy a birthday gift. A sweaty, uneasy feeling surrounded a simple trip to go check out what the store was all about. Ernie recalls standing in the parking lot after he left the store for a minute wondering whether he should put the fish symbol he had just bought on his car. The battle waged. He asked himself, "Are you really going to put this fish on your car? Are you really going to do this? Are you really going to go public with this? Are you going to make this statement when you drive into work??" He looks back now and laughs, but at the time, it seemed like such a struggle.

The second test came during media day at Sahalee Country Club for the 1998 PGA Championship Golf tournament that he was broadcasting. He was getting a chance to play the course 3 months before the tournament. He was standing in his hotel room preparing to go down and meet his colleagues to play a round of golf. A thin circular band was staring at him on the dresser. This band had the initials "W.W.J.D." – which stood for the words "What Would Jesus Do?" He had purchased it at a Christian bookstore and was now facing a moment of truth, much like the fish incident at the mall. Was he going to wear it as a statement of his faith?

He slid the band over his wrist, got on the elevator, and went down to meet the rest of the group. When he saw everyone standing there ready to load up the clubs and grab a quick breakfast before playing golf, Ernie froze. In that moment, he turned around and took off the bracelet. He felt he just couldn't do this. He did not know if he was ready to reveal where he stood spiritually in the "work segment" of his life. A piercing question crossed his mind, "Are you ready to let people know who you truly are?" In that moment, he made a decision that would affect the way he lived the rest of his life. He turned around again, put the bracelet back on and walked over to greet the rest of the group. During each handshake, Ernie nervously watched everyone's reaction to the band around his wrist. He wondered, "Do they notice the bracelet? What are they thinking?" Eventually, the hesitation, anxiety, and fear passes, and a decision such as this becomes the core of your life.

It's a weird phenomenon. We become self-conscious, because we worry about what other people will think. Ernie recalls wondering what people would think about his decision to follow Jesus. He worried that people might say, "Well, I remember Ernie as the person who did this and this and this," or "I didn't know Ernie was RELIGIOUS!" We can tend to think of all the reasons God would not choose us or all of the obstacles that God cannot overcome to use us or love us and want a relationship with us. Even after a person has made a decision of faith to follow Jesus, he or she can hesitate in the moment to share the transformation that God has made in his or her life. The key to life should not be a best-kept secret. The key question is: Are you going to be authentic or ambivalent? As with many things in life, small victories can build confidence and provide us reassurance about our decisions.

The very next year, Ernie was broadcasting the PGA championship again, and golfer Payne Stewart came up to the booth to discuss his round and the course. By this time, Ernie was wearing the bracelet all the time and never taking it off. After the interview, Ernie was announcing some off-camera promos, and he felt a tug at his wrist. He glanced down, and Payne was tugging at Ernie's W.W.J.D. bracelet and giving him a big thumbs up on his way out of the booth. An encouraging word from a courageous person who had made the same decision to follow Jesus. Reassurance in the moment. A small gesture that made a big difference.

Ernie later said, "It's a funny journey. I'm sure sometimes God is just up there laughing and saying, 'Look what you're stressing over.' Or, He is sometimes saying 'This is part of the journey. If you're going to take a public stand, you will have to go through moments like this.' When you are in the public eye, it's different, because people recognize you. It is sometimes uncomfortable to make a statement of faith, but it is well worth it."

In Matthew 10:32, Jesus promises:

> *"Whoever acknowledges me before men, I will also acknowledge him before my Father in heaven."*

The Significance of a Compass

Since Ernie's decision, his wife Cheryl has always given him something on his spiritual birthday to commemorate the moment he entered into a relationship with Jesus Christ. On December 10, 2004, Ernie returned to his home after working late on an NBA telecast. For a typical NBA doubleheader on TNT, Ernie would work in the studio until around 2 a.m. and then arrive home around 3 in the morning. Ernie slept in until 10:30 a.m., woke up, and walked into the kitchen. Cheryl was not around, but in her absence was a box with a note attached to it that read:

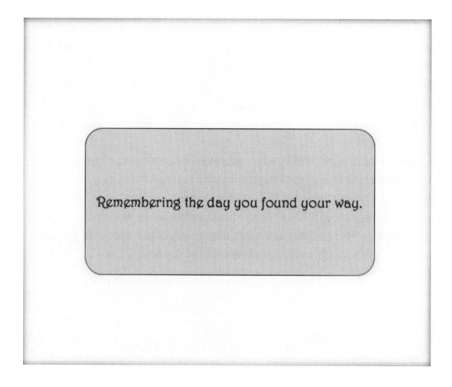

Remembering the day you found your way.

Ernie opened the box and found a compass. Ernie is not a big outdoors guy, so he knew this wasn't a tool for him to go conquer the mountains. He had already found his way and discovered an internal compass that was a lot more powerful than the one he was holding. He stood in amazement at the thought his dear wife had put into this gift. He would carry this compass with him always as a remembrance of the day he found his way on December 10, 1997. Can you think of a better way to wake up in the morning? On purpose?

What Has Become Clear?

How does God work in the midst of a trial? Why do circumstances beyond our control and reason happen to us? How do we make sense of trials we can't explain. After the diagnosis in 2003, Ernie sat down with his spiritual mentor Kevin Myers over coffee at a Starbucks to try and make sense of the situation he was in. Ernie asked Kevin at a small table at the back, "How does this work? How does God work in a situation like this? I don't want to get into a big 'Why Me?' session. But, is this punishment?" As they sat and talked, they wrote on a brown, recycled Starbucks paper napkin. Ernie still has the notes scrawled on the napkin from that day. They came back to the mantra:

The words Ernie had chosen back in 1997. Now his faith in that phrase was being tested in a major way. In situations such as these, natural feelings and piercing questions tend to burn within our hearts. Are you going to trust Him only on sunny days or when circumstances go your way? Are you going to run when the rain comes? Ernie and Kevin discussed the scenarios and his possible responses to the situation at hand. Kevin explained that it was not "Trust God if this test comes back the way I want it to" and not "Trust God if the doctor comes back with good news," but "**Trust God.... Period.**" Kevin asked him, "Are you going to trust Him in the good times, and are you going to trust Him in the bad times?"

Romans 8:28 reaffirms, "And we know that God causes all things to work together for good to those who love God, to those who are called according to His purpose."

As Ernie spoke before individuals and groups about his cancer experience, he saw God use his faith in the moment to impact people and bring glory to Him. In quiet moments alone, Ernie read about the story of Job in the Bible and discovered how God used trials and a huge personal valley for Job to bring glory to His name. That book has probably impacted more people who have gone through trials in their life than any other book in the Bible. Ernie also discovered a story in the book of John about a man who was blind. John 9:1-2 recounts that as Jesus and his disciples passed this man, the disciples asked Jesus, "Who sinned? This man or his parents, that he was born blind?" Jesus corrected them and told them they were asking the wrong question. In John 9:3 Jesus says, "Neither this man nor his parents sinned, but this happened so that the work of God might be displayed in his life."

Since reading and reflecting on the moments he has gone through, Ernie has received clarity about his circumstances. "This is not something I would have chosen for my life. Yet, through this and having this as a part of my Christian testimony has impacted people. And not because I'm any good, but because God does remarkable things through ordinary people." Ernie admits that he would not have developed this perspective if he had not made the decision on December 10, 1997, to be a follower of Jesus and to "**Trust God.... Period.**"

A Moment of Purpose

Praying in the moment had carried him through valleys and to mountaintops. A foundation had been laid in his life that would provide all the peace, courage, and focus he would ever need. It was now 2006, and Ernie was getting ready to travel an unknown path of treatment for his cancer. He had a growth on the side of his face, and people were starting to notice and wonder what was wrong. Ernie announced that he had cancer and was going to undergo treatment at the end of the 2006 NBA season.

After going through six rounds of chemotherapy treatment and losing his hair, Ernie returned to his seat in the TNT studio in the fall to serve with excellence and make an impact in the lives of other people – many he would never meet in person. In a sometimes vain industry where looks are everything, Ernie showed up with a bald head and all the confidence he needed to make it through the night. He survived the gentle jabs from former NBA player and co-host Charles Barkley and was welcomed back to his place – his sphere of influence. I'm sure that fear and doubt tried to rear their ugly heads during the summer of 2006, but Ernie never wavered in his belief that God had a plan for his life and that it was much bigger than he could have ever imagined.

"I have NO DOUBT that through the decision I made on that day in 1997, God was preparing me for the good and the bad!" Ernie exclaimed. "And God was saying, 'Realize where the credit lies, and don't get carried away with it.' Because, the old me – the pre-97 me – if I would have won an Emmy award, that would have been adding fuel to the fire." The Me-Centered fire!

Ernie won his third Emmy award in 2007 and received a chance to reveal his purpose and what brought him through these moments in his life. This would also be his first test before his peers, many of whom may not have felt the same way Ernie did about his faith. Would he trust God in the moment? Would he reveal the true source of his strength and the foundation for his life – every part of his life? And as for the credit, would he be a giver or a taker? He acknowledged that a lot of people had probably voted for him because of the cancer experience, but he saw this as an opportunity to acknowledge God in the moment.

It all came back to the phony nose and glasses. Would he put these on and hide behind a persona of me, me, me, and exclamations of look what I did? Or, would he be genuine and authentic? Would he take off the mask and reveal his true identity? Ernie was the last person to receive his award. As the applause died down, he began to speak. "Look, it's been a tough year! The only way I've gotten through this is my faith in Jesus Christ and trusting God. His hand has been on my shoulder the entire time, and, sometimes He whispers and sometime He shouts it at me. But in every moment He is telling me His plan for my life is so much better than anything I could come up with."

Before 1997, Ernie could never have imagined himself saying these words before broadcasters – people who work in his business. God gives all of us platforms – spheres of influence to impact the world. Ernie Johnson has a very public stage. For others, it may be a very private platform. Whatever your audience – whether it be 1, 100, or 1 million – you have an opportunity to influence and impact people. The question is not if, but how.

During this moment on a stage before a lot of people, Ernie publicly removed the phony nose and glasses and revealed his true identity. He admits that he struggles with the creative tension of living a spiritual life in a secular world. At times, he has wondered whether he should do something else, something more spiritual and Christian-oriented. He has come to realize that God uses people in all walks of life. God needs people everywhere to be a part of His plan, to accomplish His calling for their lives, and to be Jesus to people.

Availability and obedience. Are you living your life the way it was intended? For some of you, you have made the same decision Ernie Johnson made to be a follower of Jesus; yet you are struggling and hiding behind a mask at work or with certain people or in specific situations. We are called to be authentic, not hypocritical. Why would you waste any moment you have to pursue a life full of opportunity to impact people in the most meaningful way you can? The key is realizing that God has called you to a mission, given you moments, and placed you in roles that have a sphere of influence. The key question is what are you doing with the opportunity before you?

Ernie reflected, "From cancer to winning an Emmy award, there is no way I do this without Jesus Christ. From a moment of questioning whether I should wear the 'What Would Jesus Do?' bracelet to a platform of acknowledging my faith in Jesus Christ before thousands of people. You don't always put the pieces together of your life, or know why certain events happen, but the dominoes start to fall in place once you surrender it all and say: 'It's not about me, and it's all about you God.' I look back to that date in 1997, and see the events of my life as a seemingly-chaotic, but always glorious mixture of moments. It's fun just watching God be God!"

Ephesians 3:20-22 says:

"Now to Him who is able to do immeasurably more than all we ask or imagine, according to His power that is at work within us, to Him be glory in the church and in Christ Jesus throughout all generations, for ever and ever! Amen."

Our best-laid plans pale in comparison to what God has in store for those who trust Him. Even the smartest, most-talented person cannot out-dream God. He wants to do immeasurably more than you could ever imagine. The choice is up to you. Will you let Him accomplish His purposes in you? Will you make the same decision Ernie made?

"Live your life the way you say you live your life now!" encourages Ernie. "You don't always know the impact. And I don't think you need to know as long you are truthful to the stand you are making. Just by living your life you might impact someone. I read a quote the other day that said, 'We're planting sequoias.' Sequoias take forever to bloom, and you may never see the final result. And that's not necessary. You don't need to see the result. You just need to be there and be available.

"You can't try too hard. I don't think you can go into a day saying, 'I'm really going to make a mark today!' All you can do is to live your life. And now, I live a life that is Christ-centered instead of me-centered. Now when people ask me, 'How are you doing today Ernie?', I say, 'I'm blessed beyond recognition!' I don't even recognize that other guy – the pre-97 guy."

Ernie's advice to those of us wanting to be authentic and true to who we really are and to those of us who really want to make the most of the moments in our lives on this earth: "Seek the truth. Ask these questions:

- Am I living a charade?
- What am I looking for?
- Am I hiding behind phrases such as 'I'm a successful person' or 'I'm a great mom or dad' or 'I'm a happily married person?'
- Are you trying to put on a certain image?
- What is the truth?"

These are the questions that truly led Ernie on his journey to discover his true self. And the irony is, he didn't even know he had lost himself among the fame, the accolades, and the great marriage and family. "When you seek the truth in your life and fight through the barriers that you have built up and hid behind, it is a very freeing thing," says Ernie. "That is what enabled me to surrender everything to Jesus Christ. I don't want to live like everything is great and like I'm totally satisfied and that I've got it all together. I don't! The search for truth led me to who I really am and that's a child of God."

A Call to Action

You have reached the end of the book, and the next steps are up to you. My prayer is that the words written in this book have served as an inspiration for you to live a fully engaged life. As you read each chapter, you may have laughed, cried, been convicted, been encouraged, but most of all been inspired to a call to action. I have created this last section of the book as a resource to help you put the principles and concepts into practice in your life.

Core Concepts

Here are some core concepts to remember:

- A moment can represent a split-second instant or a longer period of time like a season of life or your whole life.
- Your choices, attitude, and response in a split-second moment can impact a generation to come – Choose Wisely!
- God has a purpose and plan for your life – you can choose to ignore, reject, or embrace this plan.
- Focus is fueled by passion and purpose.
- You can't always predict the timing of defining moments in your life, but you can be prepared for them.
- Preparation begins with an expectancy that your life has meaning and that there is a plan for you life.
- Defining moments bring clarity and confidence about your path forward.
- Perseverance and faith sustain you through valley moments.
- Embracing the journey is as important as accomplishing the goal. Don't go through the experience but miss the meaning.
- Make memories, not regrets.

- Learn from the past, prepare for the future, perform in the moment!

Six Principles

The six principles for making your life count for what matters most are:

1. **Focus on the Moment**
   To have focus in the moment, you must focus on the moment. Realize what's at stake, who else is impacted, and how you can make an impact.
2. **Enjoy the Moment**
   Embrace the journey, love who you are, and love what you do.
3. **Respond in the Moment**
   Gain perspective and choose a response of perseverance, relentlessness, and impact. Don't allow circumstances to dictate your outlook on life and your opinion of God.
4. **Perform in the Moment**
   Execute the plan!
5. **Engage in the Moment**
   Bring your whole, true self to every moment. Unleash the essence of who you are in everything you do.
6. **Pray in the Moment**
   Discover your purpose, seek God's guidance in the journey, and converse with the One who designed you.

Key Questions

Here is a summary of key questions to consider:

Chapter 1: The Meaning of a Moment

- What is the highest and best use of myself?
- Would I live my life differently if I knew I only had a short time to live?

- What is the most important thing I can do in this moment?
- What is the purpose of this moment?
- Who else is impacted by this moment?
- How do I respond in this moment?
- What choices do I make in the moment?
- How do my decisions and choices affect the outcome of a moment?
- Do I always make the best choices when confronted with a moment?
- What is my attitude in a difficult or challenging moment?
- How would other people describe my attitude?
- How do I respond to challenging situations?
- Am I an "I WILL" or an "I won't" person?
- What does patience have to do with my response in a moment?

Chapter 2: A Defining Moment

- Why do I have the platform (i.e. title, role, sphere of influence) that I have?
- What am I doing with that sphere of influence?
- Who is being impacted by my platform?
- How are they being impacted?
- How am I preparing for the defining moments in my life?
- When I think about my entire life as a "moment" in time, how have I prepared myself to focus on the "moment?"

Chapter 3: A Missing Moment

- What is my deepest fear?
- What am I doing to improve my today and impact my tomorrow?

Chapter 4: A Disappearing Moment

- Do I disappear in a moment?
- Who am I?
- What is my purpose in life?
- Why am I here?

- What is the point of my life?
- Am I making a difference?
- Am I adding value?

Chapter 5: A Mountaintop Moment

- What did it take for me to reach my goals?
- Who has helped me along the way?
- Who is being impacted by my journey?
- How is my journey affecting my growth as a person?
- Do I love my work?
- What are my strengths and talents?
- What do those who know me best say my strengths and talents are?
- What am I really passionate about?
- Do my strengths, talents, and passions line up with what I am currently doing?
- Am I fully engaged in my work?
- On Monday morning, do I have a yearning that I MUST be there?
- Do I make a positive impact?
- What is the purpose of this moment?
- What am I supposed to do in this moment?
- Who am I supposed to be in this moment?
- Who else is impacted by this moment?
- How can I grow in this moment?
- How can God be glorified in this moment?
- Why did this moment occur?
- What led to this moment?
- What did I learn from the experience of this moment?
- Am I a better person because of this moment?
- What will I do differently as a result of this moment?
- What will I continue doing as a result of this moment?
- Did I impact people in a positive way during this moment?
- Did I say the right words, do the right things, and be the right person in the moment?
- What has become clear to me as a result of this moment?

Chapter 6: A Valley Moment

- What am I doing here – physically, mentally, emotionally, spiritually?
- Does my past weigh me down?
- Is the past a stumbling block or a tipping point for me?
- Does my past work as an ally or adversary?
- What? – What do you want me to do?
- Where? – Where do you want me to go?
- Who? – Who do you want me to meet?
- How? – How should I respond?

Chapter 7: A Courageous Moment

- Where does my courage come from when I need it the most?
- Who needs me to be courageous?
- How am I performing in the moment?

Chapter 8: A Powerful Moment

- How am I being responsible for the life I lead?

Chapter 9: A Purposeful Moment

- What makes me intentional in some areas of my life but less purposeful in others?
- What have I been created and placed here on this Earth to do?
- What is my purpose in life?
- What have I been called to do?
- How am I making a difference?
- What is the point of my life?
- Am I living a charade?
- What am I looking for?
- Am I hiding behind phrases such as 'I'm a successful person' or 'I'm a great mom or dad' or 'I'm a happily married person?'

- Am I trying to put on a certain image?
- Am I authentic in all of my relationships?
- What is the truth?

Now What

During the next 30 days, I am challenging you to do the following as a result of reading this book:

- Buy a journal or notebook.
- Capture 5 big ideas that you have learned as a result of reading this book that you are going to put into practice in your life.
- Answer the key questions found in this book.
- Develop a purpose statement for your life to provide a filter for how you invest your time, your talent, and your resources (e.g. *To lead a life of faithfulness by making an impact in the lives of other people*).
- Write down the roles you have in life (e.g. student, business leader, father, mother, community volunteer, athlete, son, daughter, friend, etc.)
- Write down the names of people who are impacted as a result of these roles.
- Take inventory of the roles where you are not engaging 100 percent.
- Develop some short and long term goals to live a more fully engaged life in these areas.
- Develop a weekly habit of setting goals for each of the roles you have in life.
- Identify a friend or mentor who will keep you accountable to the goals you have set for yourself.
- Send a handwritten note to 3 people who have made a difference in your life.
- Constantly ask yourself, "What has become clear to me as a result of this moment?"
- Strive to learn from the past, prepare for the future, and perform in the moment!

You have been given so many moments… but only so many moments. Who are you going to be, and what are you going to do in the moment?

Moments

Resources

If you are interested in additional information and resources to support you in your journey, I have listed some ideas below:

- **Monday Morning Moments Web Site** – A web site dedicated to support the principles, stories, questions, and core concepts found in this book. For more information, check out:
  - www.mondaymorningmoments.com

- **Mike Van Hoozer Web Site** – This is my personal web site that contains more information about me, my blog site, and additional service offerings including keynotes, retreats, athletic and corporate coaching, and consulting. For more information, check out:
  - www.mikevanhoozer.com

- **Total BEST** – Total BEST is an organization that helps individuals and organizations integrate the principles of Balance, Excellence, Service, and Truth. For more information, check out:
  - www.totalbest.com

- **Fermi Project** – The Fermi Project is a broad collective of innovators, artists, social entrepreneurs, and church and societal leaders experimenting with ways to advance the common good in culture. For more information, check out:
  - www.fermiproject.com

- **Toms Shoes** – Blake Mycoskie (whose story was featured in this book) and his company are doing incredible things to meet the needs of the world. For every shoe you buy, they will donate a pair of shoes to children in need throughout the world. Buy some today at:
  - www.tomsshoes.com

- **Spiritual Support** – For some of you, this book may have generated some additional questions about the spiritual query and craving inside of you. Check out these resources for more information:
  - www.mondaymorningmoments.org
  - *Dinner With a Perfect Stranger* – book by David Gregory
  - *When The Game Is Over, It All Goes Back In The Box* – book by John Ortberg

About the Author

Mike Van Hoozer is a gifted communicator and coach, an insightful author and consultant, and a devoted husband and father of 5 boys who has dedicated his life to making an impact in the lives of other people. Mike is a former Senior Executive with Accenture and has over 20 years of consulting experience. He has coached and consulted with every kind of organization including small startup businesses, Fortune 50 companies, churches and non-profit organizations, and professional and amateur athletes. In his work with clients, Mike focuses on helping individuals and organizations reach their maximum potential through workshops, retreats, coaching, and consulting.

Mike is a member of the National Speakers' Association and is sought out as a speaker for organizations and businesses on the topics of leadership, human performance, teamwork, bridging the generational gap, success and significance, and work/life balance. He has served as an adjunct faculty member at Baylor University teaching on the topics of organizational and human performance and leadership development and as a coach to executive MBA students at Rice University. Mike has coached and counseled over a 1000 people including business executives and entrepreneurs in the areas of executive leadership, business development, career transitions, and personal life strategies.

Mike works with amateur and professional athletes in the areas of sports psychology, peak sports performance, and career transitions. Since 2005 when they made their World Series run, he has served as a peak performance coach and Bible study leader for the Houston Astros working with players to help encourage and motivate them through the highs and lows of professional baseball and life. Mike also works with student and professional athletes across all sports to develop mental toughness and achieve a persistent, high performance mindset.

As an author, Mike has written 2 books and contributed to several other books for Pearson Publishing and Insight Publishing. He has been published in Fortune magazine and Information Week as well as several online e-zines including CNET.

Mike is married and is the "Coach" of his own Van Hoozer basketball team with 5 boys. He is the Founder and President of Van Hoozer and Associates, a leadership think tank, and also works with the Total BEST Group helping individuals and organizations pursue the disciplines of Balance, Excellence, Service, and Truth.